D0926821

BACKCOUNTRY COOKING

*Feasts
for
Hikers, Hoofers,
and
Floaters*

BACKCOUNTRY COOKING

*Feasts
for
Hikers, Hoofers,
and
Floaters*

by
Sierra Adare

tamarack books inc.

First Edition
10 9 8 7 6 5 4 3 2 1

ISBN 1–886609–02–0

The cover photos are by Jeff Corney.

Published by:
Tamarack Books, Inc.
PO Box 190313
Boise, ID 83719–0313
1–800–962–6657

Printed in the United States of America

DEDICATION

To Western Writers of America, the best organization for bringing writers and editors together.

To all the "guinea pigs" I field-tested these recipes on.

And most of all, to C.W. for all his love and support.

ACKNOWLEDGEMENTS

Several people helped make *Backcountry Cooking* a reality. Candy Moulton deserves much credit for being my sounding board, as well as supplying me with invaluable doses of both wit and wisdom! Carolyn Lampman and Richard Brubaker, who know about the writing life, kept me laughing and sane. Chris Bendlin, the "Wonder Woman" of inter-library loans, managed to track down the most obscure references for me. Chuck Coon, formerly with the Wyoming Division of Tourism, and Linda Zerke, formerly of the Hot Springs County Museum Cultural Center, tracked down some unique historic photos for me. Gwen Petersen and Jeff Corney took on the unenviable task of reading the manuscript in its roughest drafts, offering wonderful advice and suggestions.

Kathy and Mike Gear have believed in my writing ability even when I haven't. I treasure the encouragement, understanding, and support they have given me over the years.

And most of all, Kathy Gaudry, my editor and publisher, deserves a very special thanks for believing in this book and me.

TABLE OF CONTENTS

Old fashion grub line. Photo credit: Hot Springs County Museum Cultural Center.

Early style backcountry cooking.
Photo credit: Hot Springs County Museum Cultural Center.

BACKCOUNTRY COOKING

After a long day of slogging through mud up to your gaiters, the last thing you want to think about when you stagger into camp is *what am I going to fix for dinner!* But after such a day, everybody, including the cook, deserves a hearty, tasty meal that's easy to make. Hence this cookbook. *Backcountry Cooking* features a system for preparing quick, homemade meals in the field.

The secret stems from whole meal planning and packaging before the trip ever begins. You can find all the ingredients you'll need at your local grocery store. And unlike expensive, dehydrated backcountry meals purchased from an outdoor store, the meals outlined in this cookbook cost no more than the average grocery bill to feed the same number of people for the same length of time.

How it works

In each of the sections, there are daily menus, a shopping list and advanced, at-home food preparation, such as dehydrating foods for the journey, so all you have to do is prep the foods for that menu and bag them by the meal. Start this process about a month before the scheduled expedition to insure plenty of time for dehydrating foods. Drying one meal's worth of ingredients together makes packaging meals easy and convenient.

When you tackle the wilderness, a field preparation timetable guides you through what to do upon reaching the night's campsite, which dish to get on the stove first and how to maximize fuel use by "double decker cooking." The result—appealing meals in a hurry. Tips on keeping foods hot, fast rehydration, and kitchen organization smooth the flow from pack to plate—or bowl as the case may be. Usually within half an hour, starving, cranky backpackers, goatpackers, horsepackers, or canoeists become happy campers. (Ways to adapt the menu for each kind of trip follow every meal.)

A look at the recipes

After you look over the recipes and realize they contain several ingredients you may not use at home, consider this. In the backcountry, your appetite will increase. How much depends on the exertion level, altitude, and weather conditions you face. People generally need one and one-half to two pounds of food every day in the wilderness. Winter campers require two to two and one-half pounds.

If your crew eats with hearty appetites at home, you might want to do a test run. Try one or two of the menus at home (without dehydrating the ingredients first). Should every morsel disappear and the gang still wants more, increase the amounts in the recipes to accommodate.

On the other hand, don't short-change yourself by thinking you'll never be able to eat half a pound of trail food in an afternoon or finish off a dessert in the evenings. Remember, you'll be out there hauling around fifty to eighty pounds of gear, getting the most intense aerobic exercise possible climbing up and down hills or mountains, or paddling rivers. Horsepacking provides the least strenuous workout of the lot (on you), but guess who gets to lift those sixty plus pound panniers onto the sawbucks on top of a tall horse!

While we're at it, you'll also notice salt sprinkled throughout the recipes. You may not use it at home; however, in the field your body needs more salt than normal. It helps your muscles work, and the harder you exert yourself, the more you lose salt through sweating. If your diet restricts the use of salt, feel free to omit it from the recipes, but check with your doctor about carrying a shaker of salt with you into the field just in case.

Margarine may not show up often on your table at home, and if you don't mind hauling the extra weight, no-stick cooking spray can replace much of the margarine used in these recipes. Unfortunately, at high altitudes where the temperature remains cold, the propellent can get a bit uncooperative.

For winter camping, I recommend taking margarine. The fat content not only supplies energy you will need, it takes longer to digest. This helps you feel satisfied at the end of the meal. NOTE: don't take real butter into the field as it turns rancid very quickly.

Coffee is not essential in the backcountry and might be another on that list of things you don't fix at home. Nevertheless, in the field, even non-drinkers (like me) love the way it can get your day started. Carry an extra bag of sugar and powdered milk or non-dairy creamer for those who enjoy the supplemental goodies in their fresh brew.

Remember, keep food flexibility in mind. As the food

coordinator, you should find out your crew's likes and dislikes, the amount of food and beverages they normally consume, if anybody is on a special diet, and plan accordingly.
The key is variety and enjoyment, so substitute ingredients or
have alternatives available in the field. I personally can't
stand peanut butter, but it shows up in some of my recipes.
Kids generally love it, and it provides great stick-with-you
energy. So I tuck alternative foods into my pack and eat them
while the others munch on peanut butter treats.

Dehydrating foods. Photo credit: Sierra Adare.

Dehydrating foods without special equipment

You don't need any special, expensive equipment to dry
the foods found in this cookbook.

Over the years, I've utilized every method available to
dehydrate every food imaginable. Sun drying tends to bleach
out the color of food. Wood cookstoves work grand in cold
winter months. A gas stove with a pilot light maintains a
great, low drying temperature. An electric oven or a gas range
without a pilot light takes more fiddling.

The *Backcountry Cooking* method works with all these types of ovens. For making jerky, drying ground meat, rice, chopped onion, and any other small or drippy foods, line your oven racks with foil, shiny side down. Then on goes the food with air space between each piece. Put the racks in the two slots farthermost from the heat source. Set the temperature on the lowest setting (or with just the pilot light if your stove has one). Prop the door open if food seems to be cooking rather than just drying out. (Watch the food more closely if you have an electric stove or a gas oven without pilot lights since their lowest setting tends to be a bit warm for dehydrating fruits and vegetables.) Check the food occasionally, turning it over often.

Depending on weather conditions (rainy or humid days retard the drying process), most foods will dry within twenty-four hours. Jerky, if sliced thin, should take no more than a day and a half. Unless drying meat, you can usually turn the oven off and shut the door overnight. Jerky is easiest to make if you put the meat in the oven just before bedtime. It's ready to turn over by the time you get up the next morning and generally dry by evening.

One of the best tips I've ever come across for successful jerky making is to partially freeze the meat first, then slice it. This allows you to slice it nice and thin for uniform drying. Another involves the marinating process which applies to meat or vegetables. Lay the thin slices in a glass nine by thirteen inch pan, which allows plenty of room for the ingredients. Do not use a metal pan as it may give the contents a metallic taste. Spoon marinade sparingly over the food. Add another layer of meat or vegetables and cover with marinade until you use all the ingredients. Cover with plastic and refrigerate eighteen to twenty-four hours. Do not wipe marinade off before dehydrating unless directed by the recipe.

In the recipes calling for ham and sausage, I use their

turkey equivalent. Less fat, and I prefer the taste. However, feel free to use the pork version. The at-home and in the field preparation process remains the same for turkey or pork. Grind ham or other meats by chopping it in a food processor. Or run it through a meat grinder, if you have one.

When drying fruits or vegetables, cover the oven racks with nylon netting (the coarse net, not the kind for bridal veils) purchased at a fabric store or five and dime. Then follow temperature settings mentioned above. There's no need to thaw any frozen vegetables before dehydrating. (It's usually less messy to place frozen food on the racks with air space around them than if you let food thaw first.) Use fresh fruits for drying. With the exception of blueberries, frozen fruits turn mushy and won't dehydrate as well as fresh. Dip apple, peach, and banana slices in lemon juice before drying. The ascorbic acid in lemon juice keeps these fruits from browning as they dry.

Since every oven behaves differently, experiment to see how yours works when dehydrating foods. Then note it in the cookbook for future reference.

This may sound like a lot of work, but the first time you dish up Oysters in the Mountains or Lakeside Ham with Raisin Sauce at 10,000 feet, you'll experience the art and the ecstasy of outdoor cooking!

In the field cooking techniques

Although hot water speeds the reconstituting process, waiting for water to boil consumes time and fuel. Therefore, as soon as you reach camp, add enough cold water to the bagged items to cover them, unless otherwise directed in the recipe. By the time you get the kitchen set up and make a hot drink, the rehydrated ingredients should be about ready to cook. Or better still, get a head start on the rehydrating process by adding water to the evening's meal ingredients

Cooking in the field has come a long way since this.
Photo credit: Hot Springs County Museum Cultural Center.

when you stop for a late afternoon water or snack break. (This will mean carrying some extra weight for a short while until you stop for the night.)

If foods aren't completely rehydrated by the time you set up camp and are ready to begin cooking, put them in a pot or skillet, adding water if it has all been absorbed. Cover the pot and bring to a boil. Pour in additional water as needed. Begin the cooking process once ingredients feel tender when poked with a spoon or knife.

The double decker cooking method also quickens the rehydrating process. Place the bags of rehydrating foods on top of the lid of the pot of water you're boiling for hot drinks or while cooking the main entree. A word of caution. Check occasionally to insure the lid hasn't become hot enough to start melting the plastic bags. Also, keep the bags well away from the flames.

Always cover food cooking on the stove. In addition, create a wind block around the stove by surrounding it with packs or an ensolite pad (cushioned sleeping mats purchased at outdoor stores). Be sure nothing rests so close to the stove that it can catch fire. These procedures reduce cooking time and fuel consumption.

Wasn't it Albert Einstein who said "time is relative?" That applies to backcountry cooking. Since cooking time varies, depending on altitude and weather conditions, rely more on how the food looks and feels when poked with a spoon or knife to judge doneness. Maybe the recipe said the beans should have reached a mushy consistency twenty minutes ago. But they are still hard. Keep cooking them. If the edge of the brownies or cake has separated from the rim of the skillet and the center springs back when lightly touched, they are done—even though the recipe calls for ten more minutes of baking time.

To bake in the wilderness you need a lid fire. Collect twigs between the size of matchsticks and pencils from a wide area. Pick up only deadfall. Do not use pieces from a live tree. While you're at it, gather some dead pine needles, leaves or bark for tinder.

Once you prepare the bread, brownies, cobbler, or cake for baking, place it on the stove over a low heat. The pot or skillet should never be filled to the point the food will touch the lid during the baking process. Usually you shouldn't fill the pan any higher than half way before baking.

Arrange the tinder on the lid. Loosely cover it with dry matchstick-sized twigs in a rough pyramid shape. Hold the flame of either a lighter or a match to the tinder until it catches fire. Add slightly larger twigs as the smaller ones start to burn well.

After the fire gets going, distribute it evenly over the entire surface of the lid (for even baking). Replenish the twigs as needed. The flames should feel quite hot (but not to the point it burns) when you hold your hand about six inches above the fire.

Rotate the skillet or pot during the baking process to keep food from burning. Accomplish this by placing it slightly off center over the flame. Every few minutes shift the position so another section becomes off center from the flame. An easy way to keep track of where you began the rotation is to place a rock on the ground at the starting point.

For baking times of twenty minutes or less, five minutes per quarter (once around the rotation) is fine. When the recipe calls for longer cooking, divide the baking time by eight so the food goes through two full rotations.

Allow baked items to cook at least half of the time specified in the recipe before checking on it. Otherwise the stuff may crater and never rise again. (If the leavening agent such as baking powder gets disturbed in the early stage of cooking, it goes flat kind of like an open can of soda pop left on the kitchen counter too long.)

When you do check on the food, let the fire burn to ashes, douse the lid with water, then gently brush the ashes (with a gloved hand) off the lid. Insure no live coals land on the ground that could start a fire. After you inspect the food, resume baking by creating a new lid fire, repeating this process until the food is done.

Check with the Forest Service to insure a lid fire (or a camp fire) is allowed in the areas you plan to travel through. If restrictions apply or twigs aren't available, baked items can be cooked like pancakes, flipping them to cook both sides. Be sure to use no higher than a medium heat and lower it if your food starts to burn on the bottom while remaining doughy in the center.

You can keep one pot of food warm while another cooks by wrapping a piece of ensolite around the container as soon as you remove it from the stove. The ensolite pad I sleep on is actually in two sections—one long and one short. The little piece serves a duel purpose.

Leftovers can remain in the pot or skillet and reheated as part of breakfast or bagged with the trash to be carried out.

Clean-up comes easiest when done immediately after the meal. Pour warm water into the dish and use either a pine cone, a clump of course grass stems, pine needles, sand or even a snowball as a "scrub brush." Liquid soap helps eliminate food residue and grease on dishes, however, if you don't get all of it rinsed off (and that's hard to do in camping conditions) it can lead to upset stomachs.

Discard clean-up water by pouring it through a sieve to catch any food particles. Empty the sieve into one of the plastic bags the meal was packed in. Perform all kitchen clean-up at least two hundred yards from a water source to avoid contaminating it.

The camp kitchen in bear country

Check with the Forest Service to see if you should plan on bear camping in the areas you intend to travel through. It's a good practice some places in the Rockies, even though the locales haven't been designated as "bear country." (See the backpacking section.)

Include a shovel and a thirty to forty foot rope, six to eight millimeters in diameter, in your equipment list. Select a campsite away from a wild food source such as a field of berries. Look for a relatively open area, preferably elevated (as on a knoll or hill). Set up the kitchen a good one hundred yards downwind, and preferably down hill as cooler night air stays down in valleys thus helping to keep cooking smells down low, from your sleeping quarters and one hundred yards from where you plan to hang food bags. If there are no trees in the vicinity, double wrap foods in plastic bags to cut down on odors and pile duffel bags containing the food on the ground well away from cooking and sleeping localities. Two or three different piles some distance apart may salvage eatables should a bear raid occur.

Remove all items of food and things that carry an odor (toothpaste, soap, etc.) from packs containing clothing.

The easiest and safest way to hang food bags is to tie one end of the rope around a rock and place the stone in a ditty bag (small stuff sack used for storing miscellaneous items). Tie the bag closed. Have everybody stand back. Throw the bag containing the rock over a tree limb twenty to thirty feet high. Tie the food duffels on the end of the rope and hoist them up until the bottom of the bags hang fifteen feet from the ground. The tops of the food bags should also be dangling four feet below the limb they hang from.

Dig a one foot deep sump hole at least one hundred feet from the campsite. Dispose of all dish wash and rinse water, food scraps, toothpaste spit, and bodily waste in the hole. Cover the hole at night.

If you use any canned foods, be sure to burn out the cans by holding them upside down over the stove flame to destroy any residue before crushing them and packing them with the rest of the carry-out trash.

Obtain more details from your regional Forest Service office.

A *final thought*
You don't have to go backpacking, goatpacking, horse-packing or canoeing to savor these recipes! Skip the dehydrating section and fix them at home.

Backcountry kitchen equipment. Photo credit: Sierra Adare.

Equipment list
The Backcountry Kitchen (for every 4 people):
1 lightweight backpacking stove
extra fuel bottles**
small plastic funnel (for filling stove)
2 lighters
1 non-stick 10 inch skillet with lid (remove all plastic parts
    as they will melt if cooking over coals or a camp or lid
    fire)
1–3 quart pot with lid (remove all plastic parts as they will
    melt if cooking over coals or a camp or lid fire)*
1–2 quart pot with lid (remove all plastic parts as they will
    melt if cooking over coals or a camp or lid fire)*
1 plastic spatula
1 large wooden spoon
coffee sock (a cloth filter that resembles a wind sock on a
    wire handle) [A plastic one-cup cone filter holder and

paper filters can be substituted if you don't mind the extra weight and trash to be carried out.]
1 metal or plastic sieve
at least 1 pocketknife
1 pot holder or cotton gloves
1 pair aluminum pliers
1 collapsible water jug
1 flashlight with batteries
1 short section ensolite pad (cushioned sleeping mats purchased at outdoor stores)

Backcountry Backups:
camp matches in a plastic container
stove repair kit (to go with your stove brand, obtained from an outdoor store)
extra plastic bags

Eating Essentials (per person):
1–3 cup plastic bowl with tight-fitting lid
1–2 cup plastic bowl with tight-fitting lid (nests in other bowl, taking up less pack space)
1–12 ounce insulated mug with tight-fitting lid
1 spoon

Options for Goatpacking, Horsepacking, and Float Trips:
cutting board
lantern
small folding table
cast iron dutch oven and lid or second skillet with lid
a two-burner stove
plastic container designed to carry eggs in the field
can opener
grater
1 bag charcoal bricks (variety that doesn't need lighter fluid)
small shovel

Bagging by the meal saves time and trouble when cooking in the wilderness.
Photo credit: Sierra Adare.

At Home Preparation Needs:

1 box of gallon-sized zippered plastic bags
2 boxes of quart-sized zippered plastic bags
1 box vegetable zipper plastic bags (option for trips other than backpacking)
1 box foil
2 yards nylon netting (available at fabric stores)
food processor or meat grinder
food dehydrator (optional)
1 roll duct tape
7 small plastic bottles
1 plastic container with a screw-on lid (option for canoe trip)
1 box plastic wrap

If you can find pots that will nest and create a double boiler, you can often use them to cook two dishes at the same time.

**When figuring fuel consumption, plan on using one-third to one-half of a quart bottle of fuel per stove per day during summer. (Check your stove's fuel consumption rates before going into the field.) Up this to one to one and one-third quart for winter. The higher the altitude, the longer food takes to cook. Thin, dry air allows moisture to evaporate rapidly, which in turn causes water to boil at a lower temperature. Cold and wind also contribute to depleting the fuel supply at a furious rate. (See "In the field cooking techniques" for a few tricks for on the trail.)*

Measurements and terms
Abbreviations:

T.	=	tablespoon
t.	=	teaspoon
pkg.	=	package
lb.	=	pound
c.	=	cup
pt.	=	pint
qt.	=	quart

Terms:

Bake: Cook by means of a low flame on the stove and a lid fire. (See Lid Fire.)

Cut margarine into flour: Distribute margarine thoroughly into dry ingredients by literally cutting it in with the handles of two spoons or with two pocketknives, using a scissors motion, until the margarine becomes tiny beads coated completely with flour. (The dry ingredients will resemble rough cornmeal.)

Double decker cooking method: Rehydrating a bag of

food on top of the lid of a pot containing food or water that is cooking on the stove.

Full boil: The entire surface of the water or liquid is bubbling in an agitated manner.

Lid fire: A small fire, using twigs no larger than a pencil, maintained on top of the skillet or pot lid in order to create a top heat source for baking. (See "In the field cooking techniques.")

Low boil: Surface of the water or liquid just starting to become agitated.

Sauté: Using a small amount of margarine to lightly fry meat or vegetables, stirring frequently.

Simmer: Below boiling stage. Small bubbles and steam may rise, but the surface remains calm.

Unless otherwise stated, all recipes serve three to four people.

Helpful hints

Since many recipes call for small quantities of margarine, it's more practical to add up the total amount of margarine used on the trip and bag it altogether. Then in the field, measure out the portion needed for the individual recipe. A trick you can use to keep this process from becoming a mess is to grasp the bag of margarine from beneath, unzip the top, fold the plastic back over your hand (like peeling a banana) and scoop off what you need. This also applies for nut butters or any other gooey items carried into the field.

Before leaving on the trip, insulate the three cup eating bowls and lids by cutting and taping a section of ensolite pad around them. Use duct tape for durability.

When mixing any type of dough or batter, start with a small amount of water. Reseal the plastic bag. Then squeeze it gently to moisten all ingredients. Add more water as needed to obtain the right consistency. That way you don't have to worry about carrying extra flour for dough or batter that has become too runny. If dough appears too crumbly, alternately add one tablespoon water and one tablespoon melted margarine until dough holds together.

Warm water works best when mixing dough or batter. It aids the raising of breads and cakes. Cold water can be used, but breads take longer and won't raise as well.

Accurately measuring water in the field starts at home. Measure water a quarter cup at a time into your two cup bowl, marking the level with a permanent marker.

Potatoes dehydrate easier if peeled before slicing or grating.

If you can't find fresh green chiles, drain canned ones well, pat them between a couple of paper towels, then dehydrate.

Take molasses instead of a sugar-based syrup. It tastes richer and contains many necessary minerals.

When taking fresh fruits or vegetables on a float or an animal assisted trip, prevent spoilage by choosing under- or unripened pieces to be used later in the trip. By the time you need them, they will be ripe.

Water used for cooking need not be purified with iodine tablets or purification filters prior to the cooking process. All the recipes require cooking times in excess of the five minute boiling time suggested for purifying water. Water used for tea, coffee or other beverages should be boiled for five minutes before making the drinks.

When adding fruit crystals to drinking water that has been treated with iodine tablets, allow twenty minutes for the iodine to do its job before adding crystals.

It never hurts to carry an extra day or two worth of food on a trip, just to be on the safe side. Severe weather or an injury could delay you, and it's no fun to have to ration food or do without.

Unless you are hired to do the cooking on a trip, decide who will do which camp chores while the trip is still in the planning stage. A division of labor (one person cooks for the day, another fills water bottles for use in camp, another sets up the tent, etc.) makes camp life more comfortable.

Backpacking in the Rockies.
Photo credit: Jeff Corney.

TEN DAYS OF BACKPACKING MEALS

Recreational hiking is a twentieth century phenomenon. Prior to 1900, people wandered through the wilderness for very different reasons. They searched for gold, fur, meat, or a better life, and they usually had a horse, mule, oxen, wagon, or handcart to carry their supplies.

Nowadays, backpacking trips range from an overnight experience to an excursion that lasts weeks. The comfort zone, weight-wise, maxes out around ten day's worth of provisions. If you plan to be in the backcountry for a more extended period, you should consider alternative means of obtaining fresh supplies.

One way is to pack provisions in critter and weather resistant containers, then cache them along the route by either burying them or storing them in caves. Another option is to have somebody to meet you at a designated spot with rations that you have pre-packed. Many outfitters provide such services, utilizing horses, goats, snowmobiles, skis, vehicles, parachute drops, or even backpacks to get additional food to you on the trail. Be sure to check with the Forest Service first. Many areas restrict the use of caches or the type of re-ration (e.g. no vehicle re-rations in wilderness areas).

Also inquire at the Forest Service office if any of the districts you plan to journey through are bear use areas and require special camping techniques (see page 10 for more details). The Forest Service carries several brochures on traveling and camping safely in bear country.

With all this in mind, here are ten days worth of backpacking menus and meals.

Food for the trail
The bulk bins at your local supermarket provide a cornucopia of perfect trail foods. In normal hiking conditions figure on roughly half a pound of assorted trail foods per person per day. Include more salty type items such as cracker mix and corn nuts than sweets. For convenience, pre-slice the cheese to be consumed on the trail while fixing breakfast.

Each group of hikers will have its own favorites. Mixed nuts, Sierra Madre Fruitcake, and M & M chocolate candies generally disappear fast.

I usually pick up the following assortment:
        corn nuts
        pretzels
        banana chips
        dried papaya pieces

dried pineapple rings or chunks
dried apricots
dried apples
dates
assorted fruit leathers
Peanut M & Ms
Almond M & Ms
Plain M & Ms
caramels (take individual wrappers off)
licorice
yogurt balls
walnuts
cashews
sunflower seeds
pumpkin seeds
assorted hard cheeses
Triscuits (or other wheat crackers)
cracker mix
assorted jerky (see index)
Sierra Madre Fruitcake (see index)
Summer Season Fruit Mix (see index)

Supply list (10 field days)

Baking Staples:
1–10 oz. can baking powder
1–16 oz. box baking soda
2 lb. brown sugar
1 lb. buckwheat flour
1–8 oz. container cocoa
1 lb. cornmeal
1–1 lb. box cornstarch
1–5 lb. sack white flour
1–5 lb. sack whole wheat

1 loaf whole wheat bread
1–1 lb. can powdered buttermilk
1–25.6 oz. box powdered milk
1–26 oz. box salt
1 lb. powdered sugar
1–5 lb. sack sugar

Crackers/Cereals:
1 box Graham crackers
1 box Grapenuts (or other cold cereal)
1 box Malt-O-Meal (or other hot cereal)
1 box oatmeal
1 box saltine crackers

Dried Fruit/Vegetables/Nuts (in addition to trail foods):
3–2 oz. pkg. almond slivers
1 c. banana chips
2 lbs. walnuts
1–14 oz. bag coconut
1–8 oz. pkg. dates
1/3 lb. apples
1/2 lb. apricots
1/2 lb. pineapple chunks
1–1 lb. box instant potatoes
1/3 lb. papaya cubes
1–8 oz. pitted prunes
2 lb. raisins

Fresh Fruit:
2 apples
1 qt. container blueberries
1 cantaloupe
1 honeydew melon
1 lemon

6 peaches
4 pears
2 qt. strawberries
1 pt. raspberries
10 tomatoes

Fresh Vegetables:
2 bell peppers
1 lb. broccoli flower heads
1 bunch carrots
1 bunch celery
3 eggplants
3–8 oz. pkg. mushrooms
11 onions
1 pimento pepper
4 potatoes
4 zucchini

Frozen Food:
1–10 oz. pkg. corn
1–20 oz. bag green beans (or 1 lb. fresh)
1–16 oz. bag green peas
2–20 oz. bag mixed garden vegetables
1–10 oz. bag peas
1–20 oz. bag stir fry vegetables

Meat/Milk/Margarine/Cheese:
1 1/2 lbs. ground beef
2 lbs. beef roast
2 lbs. chicken breasts
2 lbs. turkey or chicken breast
2 lbs. ground turkey
3 lbs. ham
3–10 oz. cans whole oysters in water

1 lb. cheddar cheese
1/2 lb. your favorite hard cheese
1–8 oz. can Parmesan cheese
1/2 lb. Swiss cheese
3 1/4 lbs. margarine

Rice/Noodles:
1 lb. brown rice
2–5 oz. containers chow mein noodles
1–12 oz. bag egg noodles
1–12 oz. bag vegetable noodles
1 lb. white rice

Sauces & Other Mixes/Drinks/Speciality Items:
1 jar beef bouillon cubes
1 jar chicken bouillon cubes
1 lb. coffee (makes 50 regular strength cups)
1 can hazelnut flavored coffee drink
1 jar orange drink mix
50 assorted bags tea
assorted flavors of gelatin mix (including raspberry)
assorted flavors of fruit crystals
1 pt. brandy
1–6 oz. box cornbread stuffing mix
3 pkg. brown gravy mix
2 pkg. Hollandaise sauce mix
1 pkg. turkey gravy mix
1 pkg. instant butterscotch pudding mix
1 pkg. tapioca
1 box instant cheesecake mix
1–12 oz. bag semi-sweet chocolate chips
1 bottle molasses
1 bottle soy sauce

Spices:
1 container allspice
1 container anise seed
1 container basil
1 container black pepper
1 container cayenne pepper
1 container celery salt
1 container chili powder
1 container Chinese Five Spice
1 container cinnamon
1 container cream of tartar
1 container dry mustard
1 container garlic powder
1 container ginger
1 container ground cardamom
1 container ground cloves
1 container ground coriander seed
1 container hickory smoke salt
1 container mace
1 container nutmeg
1 container onion powder
1 container orange peel
1 container parsley flakes
1 container thyme
1 bottle Tabasco
1 bottle Worcestershire Sauce

Trail Mix:
1/2 lb. per person per day (see list on page 20)

DAY ONE

BREAKFAST

Big Sandy Fry Bread with Spicy Sugar
Cheese
Coffee Sock Coffee

TRAIL LUNCH

Jerky Pingora Style
Corn Nuts
Sierra Madre Fruitcake
Plain M & Ms

DINNER

Lakeside Ham with Raisin Sauce over Rice
Mixed Garden Vegetables
First Night Cake
Tea

DAY ONE

The early July sunshine burns the chill out of the morning air as we stuff gear in our backpacks at the Big Sandy Opening in Wyoming's Wind River Range. Jeff, a veteran hiker, helps his dad, Dick, adjust the straps on his external frame pack. This will be the first time the two hike together in the Rockies. They ask me to coordinate the food and be the "official" cook on this trek to two destinations (in opposite directions), plus lots of picture-taking in between.

In preparation, I confirm the food likes and dislikes and plan the meals accordingly. Since we all enjoy a few fireworks to start off the day, jalapeno cheese accompanies our trailhead breakfast. I also include a selection of gourmet-flavored coffees which the guys enjoy drinking at home. Making camp coffee is like stepping back a century when it comes to brewing techniques.

In the 1800s, cooks used a strainer called a "biggin" to hold the coffee grounds. Boiling water was poured over the grounds and left to slowly filter through into a cup. Then folks diluted the beverage with either boiling milk or cream. According to *Mrs. Goodfellow's Cookery As It Should Be* (1865), coffee prepared in this manner is "nutritious and agreeable."

Day One Breakfast Recipes:

Big Sandy Fry Bread
1 1/2 c. whole wheat flour
1 1/2 c. white flour
2 t. baking powder
1 t. salt
1/3 c. margarine
At home, bag together all ingredients except margarine.

Spicy Sugar
1/2 c. brown sugar, firmly packed
1 t. ground coriander seed
1 t. allspice
1 t. ground cardamom
  Mix and bag.

Cheese
  Pick your favorite cheese for this breakfast or mix and match according to your backpacking group's taste preferences. You'll need about 1/2 lb.

Coffee Sock Coffee
1 T. ground coffee per cup of hot water
  Bag coffee for the entire trip in a zipper bag. Use a tablespoon at a time.

In the field preparation
  You can find quite a few currant bushes in the backcountry, but they don't produce the right kind of currant for a coffeepot. So to make coffee using a sock, bring a covered pot of water to boil over high heat. Collect all the mugs. Pour grounds into the sock. Hold it over a mug. Slowly pour boiling water through it until the mug is almost full. Add another tablespoon of coffee and repeat until everybody has some. Have sugar and powdered milk or non-dairy creamer for those who like these supplements in their coffee.
  Once the coffee is made, pour enough cold water into the bag of fry bread mix to completely moisten the flour mixture. Reseal bag and gently squeeze it in your hands until well blended. Dough should be soft, but not sticky.
  Melt enough margarine in the skillet to coat the bottom. Tear off a piece of dough and pat it between your palms until thin like a tortilla. Lay it in the skillet. Cover and cook over

medium heat. Once the bottom side cooks and begins to brown and top bubbles up, flip it to cook the other side. Repeat until all dough is cooked. Makes 10–12. Sprinkle with Spicy Sugar and serve.

THIS MEAL requires no adaptation in order to use on any of the other types of trips.

The Big Sandy River cuts through a narrow valley accented with wild flowers. Chunks of granitic rock, mottled with lichen squat beside the river. One piece, about the size of a backyard patio, provides a welcome perch for lunch. We unsling our packs, rub our aching shoulders, and climb onto the sun-basked surface.

I fish around in the top pouch of my pack, extracting the afternoon's lunchables. Since we each chugged down a quart water on the morning's hike, Dick and Jeff take our empty bottles to the river and fill them, adding an iodine tablet to each one to safeguard against water-borne parasites. However, it flavors the water like rusty pipes. After waiting twenty minutes for the iodine to do its job, we disguise the mineral taste by sprinkling some instant lemonade crystals in the bottle and shaking it well before taking a sip.

Pioneers on the Oregon Trail, which lies approximately fifty miles from our position as the raven flies, concocted their own version of "lemonade" to cover the poor taste of water. They mixed in a bit of sugar, vinegar, and lemon extract to pep it up.

Our substitute lemonade quenches our thirst while we make inroads into the mixture of sweet and salty trail foods. By the time we lie back, satiated, to let the rock's warmth absorb into our achy backs, we've wolfed down the entire bag of fruit-cake. It, like the bulk of the foods on today's menu, weighs more than the foods scheduled for later in the journey. The heavy to light rule is something to keep in mind even on short trips.

Day One Trail Lunch Recipes:

Jerky Pingora Style
1 lb. beef roast, sliced thin
1/4 c. soy sauce
3 T. Worcestershire sauce
2 T. hickory smoke salt
1 t. garlic powder
1 t. salt
1 t. onion powder
1 t. ginger
1 t. Tabasco
1 t. chili powder
    Partially freeze the roast. This makes it easier to cut into thinner strips, which in turn allows for faster and more uniform drying. Mix together remaining ingredients. Lay the strips of beef in a glass 9 x 13 inch pan. Avoid using a metal dish as it might give the meat a metallic taste. The larger surface area of this size pan allows you to distribute the marinade sauce more evenly. Spoon the marinade over the meat. Repeat with another layer. Cover with plastic wrap. Marinate 24 hours in the refrigerator. Spread the slices on a foil-lined oven rack and dehydrate.

Sierra Madre Fruitcake
3 c. raisins
2 c. pitted prunes
1 c. dried apricots
1 c. coconut flakes
2 c. chopped walnuts
1 c. banana chips
1 c. dried pineapple chunks
1 c. dried apples
brandy

Grind the dried fruits and nuts in a food processor or put them through a meat grinder. Mix fruits in a bowl with enough brandy to hold the mixture together. Pack into 2 ungreased loaf pans. Do not cover. Do not refrigerate. Let sit overnight. Then slice the fruitcake and store it in plastic zipper bags.

By late afternoon we skirt around the edge of Big Sandy Lake. I drink the last of my lemonade and get a fresh supply of water from one of four creeks that flow into the lake, not adding fruit crystals this time. While Jeff and Dick look over the map, I remove tonight's dinner bag from my pack and pour some of my water into the ham and vegetable bags. Resealing them, I store our hydrating dinner in the top pouch.

We decide to camp above the back side of the lake. This means traversing a large marshy area. Ground gives way beneath each step like walking on a suspension bridge. Rivulets of icy water crisscross the open field. Pale yellow globeflowers and white marsh marigolds push through patches of unmelted snow, the result of the Fourth of July storm.

On a pine-covered knoll three hundred yards from the lake, we discover an ideal campsite—a split-level. On the upper bench a nice slab of rock nudges out of the soil to furnish a relatively flat surface for the stove. A couple of well placed boulders assist in blocking the breeze. Trees nearby oblige as backrests while eating. Fifteen yards below lays a relatively flat, open piece of pine needle-littered duff ground.

Jeff digs the collapsible jug out of his pack and heads for the water. Dick gathers everybody's bedding, laying it out in the sleeping area. Meanwhile, I set up the kitchen.

After stacking the duffel bags containing extra clothing and gear in a semi-circle around the stove to create a wind shield, I unpack the food bags and check on the ham and vegetables. They have absorbed all the water I added earlier, but aren't completely rehydrated. I add more liquid from my drinking bottle.

By this time Jeff returns. I fuel the stove and put a pot of water on for tea. Boiling mountain creek or lake water for five minutes will kill parasites (allow a little longer at higher altitudes), so fresh, non-treated, water can be used for cooking and baking.

While the water heats, the three of us scout around for dead pine needles and twigs for the lid fire for our First Night Cake.

Pioneers went to great lengths to insure the fat or butter they cooked with didn't ruin. They packed bacon and ham in strong sacks, placed them in boxes and stuffed bran around the meat. Since butter turned rancid quickly, they clarified it by melting it. When it boiled, cooks skimmed off the scum that rose to the top until only a clear oil remained. This was poured into a tin canister and soldered shut. Randolph Marcy wrote in *The Prairie Traveler* (1859) that butter thus preserved "is found to keep sweet for a great length of time, and its flavor is but little impaired by the process."

Day One Dinner Recipes:

Lakeside Ham with Raisin Sauce
12 slices ham, ground
1 c. raisins
2 c. brown sugar, firmly packed
2 t. cinnamon
1 t. allspice
1 t. mace
1 t. ground cloves
2 t. powdered mustard

Cut fully cooked ham slices in your normal serving portions, then grind them in a food processor or meat grinder. Dehydrate ham and bag. Mix remaining ingredients and bag.

Rice
1 1/2 c. white rice
1 1/2 c. water
In a covered pot, bring rice and water to a boil. Add 1/3 c. more cold water. Simmer, covered, 20 to 25 minutes. When cooked, spread on foil-covered oven racks and dry.

Mixed Garden Vegetables
1 1/3–20 oz. bags of frozen mixed garden vegetables
Spread on foil-covered oven racks and dry. No need to thaw first.

First Night Cake
1 c. flour
1/2 c. brown sugar, firmly packed
1/2 t. allspice
1/2 t. nutmeg
1/2 t. ginger
1 t. anise seed
1 t. baking powder
1 t. baking soda
1 t. salt
1/2 c. raisins
1/2 c. oatmeal
1/2 c. plus 2 T. margarine
Mix together and bag all ingredients except margarine.

In the field preparation
As soon as you reach the night's camping spot, pour enough cold water into the bags of ham and mixed vegetables

to cover the ingredients and reseal (if you haven't started the hydration process on the trail). Do not add cold water to the rice, sauce, or cake mix.

Meanwhile, put a large covered pot of water on the stove for hot tea. Bring to a boil over high heat while you collect everybody's mug and big insulated bowl and lid. Then gather dry, dead leaves or pine needles and small twigs for the lid fire. Locate your lighter.

Divide rice between the four bowls. When water boils, pour 1/3 c. of the boiling water over each bowl of rice. Put the lids on and set aside. The rice needs at least 8–10 minutes to reconstitute.

Once you've made a mug of tea for everybody, pour the soaking ham into the pot and set aside. Pour the mixed vegetables into the saucepan. Cover and bring to a boil over high heat. As soon as they are at a full boil, remove from the stove. Put the ham over the flame. Add sauce mix and 2 c. cold water. Cover and bring to a boil. Employ the double-decker method to keep the vegetables hot while the ham cooks. When it starts to boil, reduce to low heat and simmer until meat and vegetables are tender (approximately 20 minutes, depending on altitude). Stir ham frequently. Add more water if sauce becomes too thick. It should have the consistency of syrup.

If vegetables aren't completely tender when ham is cooked, bring them to boil while you serve the ham over the rice.

During dinner, melt 1/2 c. margarine in a large pot over medium heat (no need to clean it out after cooking ham). Remove from heat. Add cake mix and 2 T. cold water. Blend until dry ingredients are moistened, adding a splash more water if necessary to form a stiff dough. Melt remaining margarine in the skillet, swirling to coat bottom and sides. Pat dough into skillet. Bake over low heat and a lid fire 40–45 minutes, rotating pan to keep the cake from burning.

When cake is done, put a covered pot of water on to boil, for another round of tea and for wash-up. AS AN OPTION on goat, horse, or float trips, pack frozen ham steaks instead of drying them. Canned mixed vegetables can also replace dehydrated ones. NOTE: on goat trips, carrying the heavier fresh, frozen, or canned foods will mean bringing an additional goat to accommodate the extra weight.

We can't finish off the cake, so I put the leftovers in a clean plastic bag and put it in my pack to have handy for trail food tomorrow.

After a last round of tea, Dick collects the dishes. Any scraps of food get scraped into one of the empty plastic bags from dinner. Next he swirls hot water in each container, using a pinecone or a clump of pine needles to scrub out the dishes. Jeff holds the sieve, and Dick strain the wash water through it to catch any food particles loosened by the scrub brush. He dumps the contents of the sieve into the scrap bag. Then they rinse the dishes in hot water and store them in a duffel. A quick check of tomorrow's breakfast menu shows nothing that needs to be soaked overnight.

DAY TWO

BREAKFAST

Mountain Gruel
Coffee

TRAIL LUNCH

Cheese
Triscuits
Dried Apples
Peanut M & Ms

DINNER

Switchback
Bridger Buttermilk Brownies
Tea

DAY TWO

People used to refer to cereals by the unflattering name of "gruel." Cooks prepared it by boiling water in a skillet and throwing in handfuls of oats or other grains and sometimes adding raisins. After the concoction boiled for ten minutes, they poured it in bowls, added salt, sugar, and nutmeg.

Day Two Breakfast Recipe:

Mountain Gruel
2/3 c. papaya cubes
2/3 c. nuts
1 1/3 c. malt-o-meal
3/4 c. sugar
3 T. powdered milk
1/2 t. nutmeg
Bag papaya separately from remaining ingredients.

In the field preparation

After the coffee water boils, pour 1 1/3 c. of cold water and the papaya in a pot. Cover. Bring to boil over low heat. Stir in malt-o-meal mix. Cook 1 minute. Serve with extra powdered milk if desired.

THIS MEAL requires no adaptation for the other kinds of trips.

Once we finish breakfast and do the dishes, we make a final sweep of the site, checking for any food scraps or items overlooked during packing. We erase all evidence of the camp by scattering the pine needles, pebbles, and duff soil dislodged last night in the sleeping area.

Next we hoist our packs onto our backs and recross the marsh to the base of Jackass Pass. There's a good reason this path is so named. As one story goes, in olden days, the steep, rugged route defied all means of transport except for the surefootedness of jackasses. Hikers, however, tell a different tale as the pass gains 1,000 feet in elevation in little over a mile.

Switchbacks zigzag up a sheer mountainside from the trailhead. Panting, we pause for breath several times. Our boots punch through ice-crusted snow on the trail. Patches of it intermingle with one boulder field after another—the rubble left by glaciation and erosion. We scramble over them, certain our lungs will burst.

But nature soon gives us a break, allowing us to head down a narrow corridor to the shore of North Lake. Sundance Pinnacle surges up out of the left corner of the dark blue water.

Sheltered in a nook between boulders scattered near the lake, we lunch on a variety of cheeses and crackers, M & Ms, leftover cake, and dried apple slices.

More often than not, eighteenth and nineteenth century shoppers could obtain dried apples far more readily than fresh. After the Civil War, the wife of an army officer stationed in the Dakota Territory paid the outrageous sum of twenty-five dollars to have a barrel of apples shipped to her from Oregon. Regardless of price, when an abundance of fresh could be procured, the apples were peeled, cut into quarters, strung like beads on a necklace and hung near the fireplace or kitchen stove to dry.

Oven drying is a lot easier!

Before hitting the trail again, we fill our water bottles from the confluence of North Creek and the lake. I also pour some water over the turkey and eggplant mixture for dinner.

Taking a hearty breath, the three of us traverse the rocky beach and continue the trek.

Another set of switchbacks leads up a rock-littered incline dotted with pines. Intermittent streams of sun-melted snow crisscross the path. A sheltered cavity recessed in the trees presents an adequate camping spot.

Once unpacked, I start water for tea, placing the bag of rehydrating meat and vegetables on the lid to speed up the process. I keep an eye on the bag while I collect mugs and bowls to insure it doesn't shift and get too near the flame or that the lid becomes hot enough to melt the plastic.

Day Two Dinner Recipes:

Switchback
1 lb. ground turkey
1 1/2 eggplant, chopped
4 tomatoes
1 bell pepper, chopped
1 onion
1/2 c. Parmesan cheese
3 c. egg noodles

Brown turkey then dehydrate with eggplant, tomatoes, pepper, and onion. Bag together. Put noodles and cheese into separate bags.

Bridger Buttermilk Brownies
1/4 c. cocoa
1 c. flour
1 T. hazelnut flavored coffee drink
3/4 c. sugar
1 t. baking powder
1 t. salt
2 T. powdered buttermilk
1/2 c. margarine

Mix dry ingredients. Bag together except for margarine.

In the field preparation

Upon your arrival in camp (if you haven't started the process on a trail break), pour enough cold water into the bag of dry turkey and vegetables to cover and reseal. Do not add water to the noodles.

Once everybody has a hot drink, pour the soaking turkey mixture into the pot. Cover and bring to a boil over high heat. Reduce to medium heat and cook until meat and vegetables are tender, 20–30 minutes. Stir frequently. Add more water as needed to keep meat and vegetables covered.

When turkey mixture is cooked, add enough water to cover ingredients again (if necessary) and bring back to boil over high heat. Add noodles. Cook over medium heat until noodles are done, about 10 minutes more. Stir frequently. When done, remove from heat and add cheese.

During dinner, melt 1/2 c. margarine in the skillet. Add 1 c. cold water, then pour this into the bag of brownie mix. Reseal. Squeeze gently until completely moistened. It should be a thick batter. Pour batter into the skillet. Bake over low heat with a lid fire for 45–50 minutes, rotating for even cooking.

After clean-up you can get a head start on the rehydration process for tomorrow. Check the breakfast menu and add cold water to the meat and vegetables tonight before going to bed.

AS AN OPTION on goat or horse trips, substitute a tube of frozen ground turkey, fresh eggplant and bell pepper, and 1–28 oz. can of whole tomatoes, provided this meal is prepared no later than the second day as the meat will spoil. On float trips, pack frozen turkey and fresh vegetables in an ice chest, but fix no later than three days into the journey.

DAY THREE

BREAKFAST

Packer's Ham Hashbrowns
Coffee

TRAIL LUNCH

Dried Apricots
Pretzels
Sunflower Seeds
Cashews
Yogurt Balls

DINNER

Oysters in the Mountains
Triple Sock Tapioca
Tea

DAY THREE

In the nineteenth century, people rarely ate fresh pork roast. They either cured and stored it in a salt brine (Salt Pork) or they made ham. To do this, pilgrims soaked pork roasts a couple of weeks in a mixture of salt water, sugar or molasses, and spices. Once removed from this solution, the meat hung in a smokehouse for several weeks, absorbing a thick cloud of oak, hickory, or maple smoke. Then the meat was rubbed with pepper, put in a muslin bag, and hung in a root cellar.

When cooks prepared ham, they scrapped off any mold that accumulated on the rind with a knife. Next they vigorously scrubbed the ham with soap suds and a brush, rinsed the meat in hot water and soaked it thirty-six hours (or longer for older hams) before baking it eighteen minutes for every pound of meat. Thanks to a bit of prior planning last night, I fix our Packer's Ham Hashbrowns in next to no time.

Day Three Breakfast Recipes:

Packer's Ham Hashbrowns
4 slices of ham, ground
4 potatoes, grated
2 tomatoes, chopped
1/2 t. salt
1 t. pepper
1/4 lb. cheddar cheese
2 T. margarine

Dehydrate ham, potatoes, and tomatoes. Bag ham and potatoes together. Combine salt and pepper with the tomatoes. Bag cheese separately.

In the field preparation

Rehydrate ham and vegetables while you make morning hot drinks (if you didn't start the process last night). Melt margarine in the skillet. Add ham and potatoes. Cover and fry over medium heat, flipping once as hashbrowns brown. Lay cheese on top. Cover. Reduce heat to low and cook until cheese melts. Serve with tomato on top.

AS AN OPTION on goat and horse trips, substitute canned ham and fresh potatoes. For float expeditions, substitute ham steaks that have been frozen, a 20 oz. bag of frozen hashbrowns, and fresh tomatoes. Store in an ice chest, and fix no later than the third morning.

Cirque of the Towers with Pingora on the left and Lonesome Lake to the right.
Photo credit: Sierra Adare.

Bear tracks, no more than a few hours old, punctuate the snowy edge of frozen Arrowhead Lake high along Jackass Pass. The animal had crossed the lake and wandered up and over the pass. Our tracks parallel the bear's along the thin strip of shore.

This isn't Jeff's first, and by no means closest, encounter

with members of the ursid family in areas they supposedly don't inhabit. By unanimous decision we vote to rig for bear camping when we set up tonight's bivouac.

On top of Jackass Pass, elevation 10,800 feet, we straddle the Continental Divide on a rock-strewn, wind-scoured tundra.

Seven hundred feet in the basin below, Lonesome Lake acts like a miniature reflecting pool for the surrounding peaks of the Cirque of the Towers, a collection of sheer rock faces, scarred and hollowed into a forboding semi-circle by glaciers during the Pleistocene Era.

The ridge we walk offers slender benches of land and stone that allow an escape from the relentless gale that steals our breath the instant we expel it. We drop down into the little, bowl-shaped valley. Pine trees radiate out from the perimeter of the lake well away from any bear tracks in the snow and soil, offering excellent possibilities for bear camping.

First we designate the kitchen, sleeping area, and a good location to hang the food bags. Jeff rigs the rope. Dick digs the sump hole, and I set up the kitchen.

I remove tonight's dinner and dessert bags and add water to the oysters and peas. While I prepare the meal, the guys double wrap all food items in plastic bags and have bags ready to store dishes, toothpaste, and soap in after we finish a last mug of tea and our tapioca pudding.

Back in the early 1800s, cooks reserved the term "pudding" for desserts with a flour or cornmeal base. They classified tapioca as a "jelly." It had to be soaked for five or six hours, then simmered in the same water and bits of fresh lemon peel until the liquid became quite clear, usually a couple of hours or more. A little wine, lemon juice, and sugar were then mixed with the tapioca before serving.

Day Three Dinner Recipes:

Oysters in the Mountain
3–10 oz. cans whole oysters in water
1–16 oz. bag frozen green peas
4 chicken bouillon cubes
4 T. margarine

Dumpling Mix
3 c. whole wheat flour
2 t. salt
2 t. baking powder
2 t. baking soda
6 T. powdered milk
2 T. parsley flakes
2 t. pepper
1 t. mace
1 t. nutmeg
    Dehydrate oysters and peas. Do not thaw peas before drying. Combine Dumpling Mix ingredients in a zipper plastic bag. Take the wrappers off the bouillon cubes and bag with the dried oysters. Store peas and margarine by themselves.

Triple Sock Tapioca
1/3 c. sugar
2 T. brown sugar, firmly packed
3 T. cocoa
1/2 c. raisins
4 T. tapioca
1 t. cinnamon
1/2 c. powdered milk
1/4 c. margarine
    Bag all ingredients together, except margarine.

In the field preparation

Reconstitute the oysters by filling the bag 3/4 of the way full. Reseal and set aside. Soak peas in just enough cold water to cover them. While water heats for hot drinks, cut 4 T. margarine into the dumpling mix. Add 1 1/3 to 1 1/2 c. cold water to make a stiff dough. Pour the excess oyster reconstituting liquor in the large pot, adding enough cold water to bring the liquid level to half full. Cover and bring to a boil over high heat. Form balls of dumpling mix around individual oysters. Drop dumplings in the boiling water. There should be approximate a third of the oysters left after the dough runs out. Add remaining oysters to dumplings and water. Adjust heat to maintain a low boil, cooking 15–20 minutes.

Melt 1/4 c. margarine in the smaller pot. Add 3 c. cold water and dry tapioca ingredients. Soak 5 minutes. Cover. Bring to boil over medium heat. Stir often. This is very rich!

AS AN OPTION for goat, horse, and float trips, substitute canned oysters and peas. The remaining recipes need no adaptation.

We become extra careful during clean-up to insure that no food particles remain in the dishes or land on the ground. All waste products go in the sump hole, which we cover with dirt for the night. Next we stow all the food, cooking utensils, dishes, toothpaste, and soap in duffels and haul everything over to the hanging site. It takes the three of us to hoist it.

DAY FOUR

BREAKFAST

Flapjacks
Coffee

TRAIL LUNCH

C.W.'s Turkey Jerky
Cracker Mix
Dates
Almond M & Ms

DINNER

Rapid Trail
Boot Wax Apples

DAY FOUR

Pilgrims and pioneers relished the taste of griddle cakes made with what they called "Indian meal." Stirring up cornmeal, sour milk, saleratus (a kind of baking soda), and sugar, camp cooks would start flipping flapjacks before dawn to satisfy the hungry appetites of field hands. Because breakfast was often the only meal served as part of a hired hand's "room and board," women's journals recorded fixing the men twenty to thirty flapjacks apiece. One frustrated cook gave out after a worker came back for his seventy-fourth flapjack.

Day Four Breakfast Recipe:

Flapjacks
1 1/2 c. cornmeal
1 c. flour
1 t. baking powder
1 t. salt
1/4 c. sugar
1/4 c. powdered milk
6 T. margarine
   Bag together all ingredients except margarine.

In the field preparation

Melt 3 T. margarine in the skillet. Add it and 1 c. cold water to bag of dry ingredients. Reseal and gently squeeze to moisten. Add more water if need. It should pour into the skillet as a thick batter. Melt enough of remaining margarine to lightly coat the bottom of the skillet. Pour in some batter, cover, and cook until tops are firm and undersides brown. Flip. Repeat until all batter is used. Makes 12–16, depending on size of cakes. Serve with molasses.

   THIS MEAL requires no adaptation for goat, horse, or float trips.

We camp opposite of Pingora Peak, the most prominent formation in the Cirque of the Tower. It ranks as a favorite for ambitious climbers, shooting up from Lonesome Lake like a gargantuan tree stump. Supposedly, Pingora derives its name from the Shoshone language and means "high, rocky inaccessible peak."

We break camp and zigzag back down Jackass Pass, stopping on the shore of North Lake again to lunch among the boulders, sheltered from the ever-present wind—one of the elements the Cheyenne used in drying jerky. After cutting meat into thin strips, the women laid the pieces over bushes or on a hide, letting sun and air draw the moisture out of the meat. (The chore of keeping bugs and other things away from the meat fell on the children.) Once the meat dehydrated, the women packed it in *parfleches,* boxes made from heavy buffalo rawhide convenient for packing on a horse's back.

Day Four Trail Lunch Recipe:

C.W.'s Turkey (or Chicken) Jerky
1 lb. boned turkey (or chicken breast), sliced thin
1/4 c. soy sauce
1 t. garlic powder
1 t. salt
1 t. onion powder
1 t. ginger
1 t. chili powder
1 t. basil
1 t. ground coriander seed

Partially freeze meat. Cut into thin strips. Mix together remaining ingredients. Lay strips of fowl in a glass 9 x 13 inch pan. Spoon seasoning mixture evenly over meat. Repeat with another layer. Cover with plastic wrap. Marinate 24 hours. Spread on foil-lined over rack and dehydrate.

East Temple Peak on the left. Temple Peak on the right. Photo credit: Sierra Adare.

A yellow-bellied marmot scurries out of his burrow in the rock slide and onto his observation platform, which happens to be just above our picnic area. From this pedestal, the furry little lookout scolds us for intruding. Dick gets a good picture of the marmot that keeps a wary eye on Jeff and me as we refill our water bottles for the next leg of the journey.

It's mid-afternoon by the time we reach Rapid Creek Trail which leads us to our second destination—East Temple Peak. The trail weaves among tall pines that obstruct the view of the stream running out of Rapid Lake. Sounds of gushing water meander in and out of hearing range as we progress up the steep incline.

We reach its plateau near Miller Lake and take a water break. I seize the opportunity to slip into a sweater and pull pants over my shorts, feeling the chill produced by the higher altitude. For every 1,000 feet in elevation, the temperature drops three to six degrees. A strong wind chill makes it colder still.

Even though it's been a long day, we decide to travel a bit farther. Jeff passes around some dried pineapple, known to hikers as "power rings" because they provide a quick boost of energy. Meanwhile, I add water to tonight's zucchini. By the time we make camp, we'll all be waving the hunger handkerchief—a practice of early American farm hands to signal their need for some food.

Beyond Miller Lake, the trail slants upward very gently toward Temple Lake, actually three connecting bodies of water. Rays of the setting sun shimmer on the distant, snow-frosted peaks by the time we locate a small depression in the slope above the lower end of the lake. Darkness casts its shadow as we set up our base camp at 10,600 feet elevation.

Stunted limber pines maintain a meager hold on this snow-dappled pocket of soil. Dick and Jeff anchor our fly to the sturdy tree limbs the same way Plains Indians tied a cloth or hide canopy between trees for protection from the elements. I arrange the packs around a rock outcropping to form a wind shield for the kitchen area.

Home for two nights!

Our appetite hardly allows us to wait for the cheese to melt over the zucchini and cracker mixture. Crackers, and their harder, heavier counterpart hardtack, graced many a pioneer meal. Oregon Trail traveler Ellen Toole wrote in her diary, "Had ham, dried beef, crackers, pickle and syrup for dinner with brandy today."

Many women baked a supply of crackers before leaving for the West and packed them in boxes for the trip. They made them by combining a pound of flour, a pinch each of cream of tartar and saleratus, and two ounces of fresh butter with enough milk to form a stiff paste. Next the women beat the mixture smooth with a rolling pin, then rolled the dough out very thin. After cutting the crackers in squares and pricking each with a fork, the cook transferred the squares to a cookie tin and baked them in a hot oven.

Day Four Dinner Recipes:

Rapid Trail
4 medium zucchini, sliced thin
2 onions, diced
1 bell pepper, chopped
1 c. Swiss cheese, grated
12 mushrooms, sliced
1 pimento pepper, chopped
1 t. cayenne pepper
1 t. black pepper
16 saltine crackers, crushed
1/4 c. margarine
     Dehydrate zucchini, onions, and peppers. Bag vegetables together. Crush crackers and bag with cayenne and black pepper. Bag cheese separately.

Boot Wax Apples
2 apples
1/3 c. sugar
1 t. cinnamon
1 pkg. instant butterscotch pudding mix
1/3 c. powdered milk
     Dehydrate apples and bag with the sugar and cinnamon. Bag pudding mix and powdered milk together.

In the field preparation
     Rehydrate vegetables and apples. Collect small bowls and lids while water boils for hot drinks. Place vegetables in the skillet. Cover. Bring to a boil over high heat. Reduce to medium and cook until tender. Once done, shove vegetables

to one side of the skillet. Add margarine. When it has melted, blend in crackers and vegetables. Add cheese and more margarine if needed. Mix thoroughly. Cover and remove from heat. Serve when cheese has melted.

While eating dinner, cook apples in sugar, cinnamon, and 1/4 c. water until it cooks down. Divide pudding mix evenly between the bowls. Add 1/2 c. of cold water per container, cover, and shake for 30 seconds. Allow pudding to sit for 5 minutes. Pour apples over pudding and serve.

AS AN OPTION on float trips, substitute fresh vegetables and store in an ice chest. Otherwise, this meal is suitable as is for other types of trips.

DAY FIVE

BREAKFAST

Orange Sunrise
Pemmican
Coffee

TRAIL LUNCH

Jerky Pingora Style
Cheese
Triscuits
Pineapple and Papaya Chunks
Mixed Nuts
Caramels
M & Ms

DINNER

Summit
Hiker's Heaven
Cold Night Hot Toddy

DAY FIVE

The morning to ascend East Temple Peak arrives, demanding a hearty, stick-with-you breakfast that begins with pemmican. Native Americans shared this recipe with settlers as a means of preserving meat and berries in a nutritious, tasty manner. Cheyenne women pounded dried meat with a stone maul on a flat rock that rested in the bottom of a dish-shaped parfleche. As the meat powdered, they add dried berries. Once this step was completed, the women removed the stone and poured melted fat and sometimes bone marrow over the mixture and served it.

Day Five Breakfast Recipes:

Orange Sunrise
2 c. flour
1/2 c. sugar
2 t. salt
2 t. allspice
2 t. baking powder
2 t. dried orange peel
4 T. orange drink mix
1/2 c. powdered milk
1/2 c. plus 1 T. margarine
    Bag all ingredients together, except margarine.

Orange Glaze
1/4 c. powdered sugar
1 T. margarine
    Bag separately.

Pemmican
1 lb. ground meat
1 pt. raspberries
4 T. margarine

Brown the ground meat. Dehydrate it and the berries. When dry, grind to a powder in a blender. Store in zipper plastic bag separate from the margarine.

In the field preparation

Melt 1/2 c. margarine in the skillet. Mix in 1/4 c. cold water. Add margarine mixture to dry Orange Sunrise ingredients. Reseal and squeeze gently until ingredients are completely moistened and mixture makes a stiff dough. Melt 1 T. margarine in the skillet, swirling to coat the bottom and sides. Pat dough into skillet. Cover and bake over low heat with lid fire for 50 minutes.

Put 4 T. margarine in the small pan. Hold over the lid fire until margarine melts. Remove from heat and add pemmican powder and mix well. Divide among the bowls and serve while the Orange Sunrise bakes.

Melt 1 T. margarine in a small pan and hold over lid fire. When melted, pour into sugar. Reseal bag and squeeze to mix. Drizzle over hot rolls. Cut into wedges and serve.

THIS MEAL requires no adaptation to be suitable for any other types of trips.

Before we load our day packs with trail foods and plenty of water, I start the rehydration process on the chicken and vegetables. We'll be in need of a fast dinner tonight.

We skirt the upper sections of Temple Lake, locked in ice. Beyond it lays a nearly vertical snowfield up the mountainside. Jeff shows Dick and me how to "kick step" our way up it by cutting into the snow with the toe and side of our boot. This creates a platform to stand on while we cut the next step.

It sounds easy, but within half an hour my calves, as well as my lungs, protest vigorously. Pausing, I lean into the slope and try to catch my breath.

Then I push on. Time is working against us. We need to reach the summit before noon because once the sun hits this snowfield head on, softening it, travel might become tricky, possibly even dangerous.

Exertion mixed with the warming day already sees us shedding our fleecy pile jackets and pants. By the second hour, fatigue sets in. Jeff heads for a patch of snow-free, boulder-cluttered ground. Springs flow and pool up in clusters of rock, ready-made fountains for our water bottles.

Reclining against boulders, we energize our bodies with extra rations of trail foods. The pineapple, caramels, and M & Ms receive the bulk of our attention.

But the sun continues to climb toward the zenith. So must we.

Light radiates scorching brightness off the snow as we get closer to our destination. The surface soon turns slick and a bit slushy beneath our boots. Near the top, the snow gives way to huge boulders precariously scattered. A stout current blows up and over the summit.

When I crawl up onto the rock at the very pinnacle of East Temple Peak, elevation 12,590 feet, a quote from a James Cagney movie leaps instantly to mind. "Top of the world, ma!"

From the summit, the heart of the Winds' high peaks, forty-three of them over 12,500 feet, commandeer the horizon. A truly awesome sight.

The ascent took over four hours. We descend in less than half that time. In a far more enjoyable manner, too. Mountaineers call it "glissading." With feet together, we squat and push off with our hands, sliding down snowfields with our hiking boots doubling for a sled. Of course, we amateurs all end up on our bottoms. And, at one point, Dick careens out of control, rumbling over me, practically slam-

ming into a boulder and winds up spinning around like a
break dancer imitating an upside down turtle!
   What a day!

Day Five Dinner Recipes:

Summit
3 chicken breasts, ground
2 onions
1–20 oz pkg. frozen stir fry vegetables
6 mushrooms
1 t. garlic powder
1 t. ginger
1 chicken bouillon cube
1 t. cornstarch
1 T. margarine
2 1/2 c. chow mein noodles
2 T. soy sauce
   Dehydrate chicken, mushrooms, stir fry vegetables, and
onions. Bag these together with bouillon cube (remove wrap-
per), garlic powder, and ginger. Keep cornstarch, noodles,
margarine, and soy sauce all separate.

Hiker's Heaven
1–12 oz. bag of semi-sweet chocolate chips
1/2 c. coconut flakes
1/2 c. almonds slivers
1/2 t. Chinese Five Spice
1 c. chow mein noodles
   Bag chocolate, coconut, nuts, and spice together. Store
noodles separately.

Cold Night Hot Toddy

1 c. powdered milk

1 T. nutmeg

4 T. margarine

Bag milk and nutmeg together and separate from margarine.

In the field preparation

Reconstitute chicken and vegetables by adding a cup more of water than it takes to cover everything. Make a hot drink. Melt margarine in skillet. Pour chicken mixture in, insuring that there is a full cup of liquid. Cover. Bring to a boil over high heat. Reduce to low and simmer until meat and vegetables are tender. Add water if needed to maintain a cup of liquid. Mix cornstarch, soy sauce, and 1/4 c. water in a plastic bag and set aside. When food is done, check fluid level and bring to boil once again. Add cornstarch mixture. Cook 1 minute, stirring constantly. Serve over chow mein noodles.

For dessert, melt chocolate mixture over low heat in pan. Collect the smaller bowls. When chocolate melts, stir in noodles. Divide among the bowls. Serve.

When ready to round off the evening, boil 4 c. water. Stir in milk mixture and margarine. Serve.

AS AN OPTION on float trips, substitute fresh chicken that has been frozen and frozen stir fry vegetables, provided this meal is cooked within the first two days of the voyage. Otherwise, substitute canned chicken, which makes this meal suitable for goat and horse trips as well.

DAY SIX

BREAKFAST

Windpants
Coffee

TRAIL LUNCH

Cashews
Pumpkin Seeds
Banana Chips
Cracker Mix
Licorice

DINNER

Hiking Hollandaise
Jerky
Day's End Cake

DAY SIX

Day Six Breakfast Recipes:

Windpants
4 pears, sliced thin
1 t. cinnamon
1 t. cayenne pepper
1 t. mace
1 t. nutmeg
1/2 c. brown sugar, packed firm
1 recipe of Mountain Baking Mix
      Dry pear slices and bag. Mix remaining ingredients together and bag.

Mountain Baking Mix
1 1/2 c. flour
1 T. baking powder
3 T. powdered milk
1 t. salt
      Mix and bag.

In the field preparation

Fill a large pot half full of cold water. Add pears and brown sugar mix. Cover and bring to a boil over high heat. Add 1 1/4 c. cold water to the dumpling mix to make a stiff dough. Reseal the bag and squeeze it between your fingers until completely mixed. Drop dough a teaspoon at a time into the boiling pears. Lower heat and simmer, covered, for 30 minutes.

AS AN OPTION on goat, horse or float trips, substitute fresh or canned pears.

Day Six Dinner Recipes:

Hiking Hollandaise

1 lb. broccoli flower heads, broken into small pieces
1 onion, chopped
12 mushrooms, sliced thin
4 stalks celery, chopped
3 c. vegetable noodles
2–1.6 oz pkg. Hollandaise Sauce Mix

Remove stems from broccoli flowers. Dehydrate along with onion, mushrooms, and celery. (Stems take much longer to rehydrate, slowing the cooking process if included.) Bag together. Bag noodles separately. Don't forget to include the 2 pkg. of sauce mix.

Day's End Cake

1 1/3 c. whole wheat flour
2/3 c. powdered sugar
1 t. salt
2/3 c. dates
1/3 c. almond slivers
1 t. cream of tartar
1/4 c. brown sugar
1 t. baking powder
1/2 c. margarine

Mix all ingredients except margarine in a zipper bag.

In the field preparation

Rehydrate vegetables by filling half the bag with cold water. Once everybody has a hot drink, pour the soaking broccoli mixture into the pot. Cover and bring to a boil over high heat. Reduce to medium heat and cook until vegetables are tender 20–30 minutes. Stir frequently. Add more water as needed to keep vegetables covered.

When broccoli mixture is cooked, add enough water to cover ingredients again (if necessary) and bring back to boil over high heat. Add noodles. Cook, covered, over medium heat until noodles are done, about 10 minutes more. Stir frequently. If there isn't a cup of liquid in the vegetable/noodle mixture, add more. Sprinkle sauce mix into ingredients. Cook, stirring constantly until sauce thickens. Remove from heat.

Melt 1/2 c. margarine in the skillet. Add it and 1 c. water to dry cake ingredients. Mix until you have a thick batter. Pour into the skillet. Cover. Bake over low heat and a lid fire for 20–40 minutes, or until done.

AS AN OPTION on float trips, take fresh or frozen broccoli and fresh mushrooms and celery in the ice chest. For goat and horse trips follow the recipe unless this meal will be prepared the first night.

DAY SEVEN

BREAKFAST

Packframe Potato Cakes
Fruit and Nuts
Coffee

TRAIL LUNCH

C. W.'s Jerky
Pineapple Rings
Walnuts
Cracker Mix
Assorted M & Ms

DINNER

Ditty Bag
Wilderness Strawberry Cheesecake
Tea

DAY SEVEN

Day Seven Breakfast Recipe:

Packframe Potato Cakes
1 c. flour
1 c. instant potatoes
1 c. powdered milk
1 1/2 t. baking powder
2 t. salt
1/2 t. cayenne
1/4 lb. cheese, sliced
1/4 c. margarine
    Mix together all ingredients except cheese and margarine, which are bagged separately. Store in plastic bag.

In the field preparation
    While coffee water boils, pour 1 1/2 c. cold water into the bag of dry Packframe Potato Cake ingredients. Reseal bag and gently squeeze it in your hands until well blended. This will resemble a thick batter. Add more water if necessary.

    Melt enough margarine in the skillet to coat the bottom. Spoon batter into pan, forming small pancakes. Cover. Cook over low heat until cake bottoms are brown and the tops firm. Flip. Add more margarine if needed. Lay a slice of cheese on top. Cover and cook until the bottoms brown and cheese is melted. While cakes are cooking, pull out a bag of dried fruit and nuts to serve with them.

    THIS MEAL require no adaptation for other types of trips unless you care to serve fresh fruits instead of dried.

Day Seven Dinner Recipes:

Ditty Bag
1 1/2 lbs. ground beef
12 mushrooms, sliced thin
1–10 oz. pkg. frozen peas
4 large carrots, sliced
1 onion, chopped
3 c. egg noodles
1 recipe Sauce Mix
    Bag together all ingredients except egg noodles and sauce mix, which are bagged separately.

Sauce Mix
1/2 c. flour
1/2 c. powdered milk
1 T. black pepper
1 t. cayenne pepper
2 T. parsley flakes
2 t. salt
1 T. dry mustard
1 t. celery salt
1 t. thyme
1 t. garlic powder
1 t. onion powder
1 t. chili powder
    Mix together in a plastic bag. Keep sauce mix and egg noodles in separate bags.

Wilderness Strawberry Cheesecake
1 box of cheesecake mix
1/2 pt. fresh strawberries, sliced thin, then dehydrated
12 graham crackers, crushed
    Remove cheesecake mix from the box and pour into a

plastic bag. In separate bags, store strawberries and crushed crackers.

In the field preparation

Rehydrate meat and vegetables. Do not add water to the noodles or sauce mix.

Meanwhile, make tea and collect everybody's little bowl. Pour some of the crushed graham crackers into the bottom of each bowl. Add enough cold water to the cheesecake mix to completely moisten, squeezing gently to thoroughly blend. Spoon it over the crackers, dividing it evenly. Set aside.

Pour the soaking meat and vegetables into the pot. Cover and bring to a boil over high heat. Reduce to medium heat and cook 20 minutes or until meat and vegetables are tender. Stir frequently. Add more water as needed to keep meat and vegetables covered.

To rehydrate strawberry slices, cover with cold water and set bag on top of the lid of the cooking Ditty Bag. If lid becomes too hot, remove strawberries.

When the meat mixture is cooked, add enough water to cover ingredients again (if necessary) and bring to boil. Add noodles. Cook over medium heat until noodles are done, about 10 minutes. Stir frequently. Add additional water if needed to insure 1/3 inch in the bottom of the pan. Add sauce mix, stirring constantly until water is absorbed by the sauce mix and it cooks for five minutes. If sauce become too thick, thin with a bit of cold water. Serve.

During dinner, put a covered pot of water on to boil for another round of tea and for wash-up.

When ready to serve cheesecake, spoon strawberries on top and hand out.

AS AN OPTION on goat and horse trips substitute canned vegetables. On float trip, fresh frozen ground beef and fresh or frozen strawberries may be substituted if the meal is served within the first three days of the trip. Store in an ice chest.

DAY EIGHT

BREAKFAST

Boulder Field
Coffee

TRAIL LUNCH

Jerky Pingora Style
Raisins
Assorted Fruit Leathers
Yogurt Balls

DINNER

Gaiters
Wild Side Rice
Trailblazer Biscuits

DAY EIGHT

Day Eight Breakfast Recipe:

Boulder Field
4 c. Grapenuts
8 T. orange drink mix
1/3 c. powdered milk
1 c. nuts, chopped
    Bag all ingredients together.

In the field preparation
    Gather large bowls while water boils for coffee. Divide dry ingredients into bowls, add enough water to gain consistency of cereal and milk. Serve.
    THIS MEAL require no alteration for goat, horse, or float trips.

Day Eight Dinner Recipes:

Gaiters
1 eggplant, sliced thin
1 onion, chopped
8 mushrooms, sliced thin
4 tomatoes, chopped
1 t. pepper
1/2 t. garlic powder
1 t. basil
1 t. parsley flakes
1 recipe Wild Side Rice
    Dry eggplant, onion, mushrooms, and tomatoes. Bag with seasonings. Store rice separately.

Trailblazer Biscuits
1 1/3 c. flour
1/3 c. sugar
1 t. salt
1 t. baking powder
1 t. baking soda
1 t. ground coriander seed
1/4 c. powdered milk
1/4 c. plus 2 T. margarine
    Bag together all ingredients except margarine.

Strawberry Topping
1 pt. strawberries, sliced thin
1/4 c. powdered milk
    Dehydrate strawberries and bag with milk.

Wild Side Rice
1 c. brown rice
1 c. water
    In a covered medium saucepan, bring rice and water to a boil. Add 1/3 c. more cold water. Simmer, covered, 30 minutes. When cooked, spread on foil-covered oven racks and dry.

In the field preparation
    Rehydrate vegetables and Strawberry Topping. Put a pot of water on to boil. Collect large bowls. Divide rice between the four bowls. When water boils, pour 1/3 c. over each bowl of rice. Put the lids on and set aside. The rice needs at least 10–15 minutes to reconstitute.
    Place eggplant mixture and an additional 1 c. cold water in a large pot. Cover and bring to a boil over high heat. Reduce to low and simmer until tender. Serve over the rice.
    Cut 1/4 c. margarine into dry biscuit ingredients. Add

1/3 c. cold water. Reseal bag and squeeze to mix. Makes a stiff dough. Pat balls of dough into biscuits no more than 1/2 inch thick. Arrange in a skillet. Cover. Bake over low with a lid fire for 25–30 minutes. Serve with Strawberry Topping. Makes 12–15 biscuits.

AS AN OPTION on float trips, substitute fresh vegetables and tomatoes and either fresh or frozen strawberries. If this will be the first evening's meal on goat or horse trip, fresh foods may be taken. Otherwise, use this recipe on animal-assisted trips.

DAY NINE

BREAKFAST

Shorts
Coffee

TRAIL LUNCH

Cheese
Assorted Crackers
Apricots
Cashews
M & Ms

DINNER

Tent Stake Turkey
Snow Drifts

DAY NINE

Day Nine Breakfast Recipe:

Shorts
1 1/2 lb. ground beef
1 c. flour
1/3 c. buckwheat flour
1/3 c. Malt-O-Meal
1 t. baking powder
1 t. salt
5 T. powdered buttermilk
6 T. margarine
3 pkg. brown gravy mix
Brown meat. Dehydrate and bag. Bag together remaining ingredients except for margarine and gravy mix, which are stored in two separate bags.

In the field preparation

Rehydrate meat. While water boils for coffee, cut margarine into the shortcake mix. Add 3/4 c. water into the shortcake mixture. Seal bag and squeeze to moisten ingredients. Form biscuits about 1/2 inch thick. Drop into the skillet. Cover and bake with a lid fire for 25–30 minutes. Makes 20.

When done remove and set aside. In smaller pot, bring meat and enough water to cover the bottom of the pan to a boil over high heat. Cook, adding more water if necessary, until meat is tender. Add 3 c. of cold water and the gravy mix. Bring to a boil over low heat, stirring constantly. Boil for three minutes. Serve over shortcakes.

AS AN OPTION on float trips, substitute frozen ground meat stored in an ice chest. For goat and horse trips, use the frozen meat alternative only if this breakfast will be your first in the field.

Day Nine Dinner Recipes:

Tent Stake Turkey
2 lb. ground turkey
1 onion
4 stalks celery
1–20 oz. pkg. frozen green beans (or 1 lb. fresh)
1 box cornbread stuffing mix
1 pkg. turkey gravy mix
1/4 c. margarine
    Dehydrate turkey, onion, beans, and celery. Do not thaw beans first. Bag meat and vegetables with the stuffing seasoning packet. Store stuffing bread, margarine, and gravy mix in three separate bags.

Snow Drifts
1/4 c. cornstarch
3/4 c. coconut
1/2 t. cinnamon
1/4 c. powdered milk
1 t. salt
3/4 c. sugar
1/3 c. raisins (optional)
    Mix together and bag.

In the field preparation
    Reconstitute meat and vegetable mixture. Make hot drinks. Put meat mixture in the large pot. Cover and bring to a boil over high heat. Add water as it becomes absorbed.

    Pour pudding mix into a large pot. Slowly stir in 1 1/4 c. water. Cook over medium heat until mixture boils, stirring constantly. Boil 3 minutes. This is very rich!

AS AN OPTION on float trips, substitute frozen turkey and beans and fresh celery and onion. Keep the recipe as is for goat and horse trips unless it will be served the first night.

DAY TEN

BREAKFAST

Cirques
Coffee

TRAIL LUNCH

C.W.'s Jerky
Corn Nuts
Dates
Summer Season Fruit Mix
Caramels

DINNER

Rocky Mountain Trout
Moleskin Mushroom Soup
Mediterranean Vegetable Mix
Camp Comfort

DAY TEN

Day Ten Breakfast Recipe:

Cirques
4 slices ham, ground
1–10 oz. pkg. frozen corn
2 c. flour
2 t. baking powder
2 t. salt
1/2 c. powdered milk
4 T. margarine
    Dehydrate ham and corn. NOTE: do not use popcorn instead. Popcorn makes a poor substitute for sweet corn. Also, don't thaw corn before drying. Just arrange it and the ham on foil-lined oven racks. Bag together all remaining ingredients except margarine.

In the field preparation
    Rehydrate ham and corn. Double decker the bag containing ham mixture on the lid while making coffee. Pour ham mixture in the skillet and bring to a boil over high heat. Add 2 c. cold water to flour mix. Squeeze in the bag to completely moisten, making a thick batter. Add ham mixture. Melt 1 T. margarine in the skillet. Spoon fritters into it and cook, covered, over medium heat. Flip once. Repeat until all batter is used. If the outside is cooking too fast while the middle stays raw, reduce heat. Makes 20. Serve with honey if desired.
    AS AN OPTION on float trips, take fresh, frozen or canned ham and corn. Canned foods work well on the goat and horse trips.

Day Ten Trail Lunch Recipe:

Summer Season Fruit Mix
1/2 cantaloup, diced
1/2 honeydew melon, diced
2 c. blueberries
1 pt. strawberries, sliced thin
6 peaches, pitted and sliced thin
　　Dehydrate. Mix together and bag for the trail. NOTE: honeydew melon makes a delicious addition to trail food, however, when reconstituted, the flavor washes out.
　　AS AN OPTION on float trips, use fresh fruits. The recipe remains as is for goat and horse trips.

Day Ten Dinner Recipes:

Rocky Mountain Trout
1 trout, cleaned, per person
1/4 c. onion, chopped
4 slices of lemon
　　Dehydrate onion and lemon. Bag together. NOTE: if you don't plan to fish on your trip, or doubt your luck, bring along a spare dehydrated meal from the goatpacking or horsepacking sections.

Moleskin Mushroom Soup
1 onion, chopped
6 mushrooms, sliced
3 beef bouillon cubes
4 slices whole wheat bread
3 T. margarine
2 T. Parmesan cheese
　　Dehydrate onion, mushrooms, and bread slices. Bag onion, mushrooms, and bouillon cubes (remove wrappers)

together. Store margarine, bread, and cheese in three separate bags.

Mediterranean Vegetable Mix

1 1/3–20 oz. bags of frozen mixed garden vegetables
Spread on foil-covered oven racks and dry. No need to thaw first.

Camp Comfort

1–3 oz. pkg. raspberry flavored gelatin mix
1 t. cinnamon
Remove gelatin from the box and bag with cinnamon.

In the field preparation

Rehydrate onion/lemon mixture and the onion/mushroom mixture. Make hot drinks in a large pot, insuring 2 c. of water remain. Add onion/mushroom mixture. Cover and bring to a boil over high head. Reduce to medium and cook until vegetables are tender. Pour soup into large bowls. Float a piece of bread on top of each portion. Sprinkle with cheese and serve. Eat while preparing the fish and vegetables.

Bring vegetables and enough water to cover them to boil in the smaller pot over high heat. Simmer until the fish is ready to cook.

Stuff onion in trout. Lay lemon slices on top. Add 1 c. cold water. Cover and steam in the skillet 30–35 minutes. Flip fish once about half way through cooking time. Add more water if necessary.

Employ the double-decker method to keep the vegetables hot while the trout cooks. When it starts to boil, reduce to low heat and simmer until meat and vegetables are tender (approximately 20 minutes, depending on altitude). Serve.

Heat more water. Collect mugs. Spoon 2 T. of gelatin mix in each mug and add boiling water. Stir well and serve.

AS AN OPTION on goat, horse, or float trips, bring canned fish as a substitute for fresh trout and a fresh lemon. A raw onion and canned mushrooms and beef broth can replace the dried soup ingredients. A mix of fresh or frozen vegetables can replace dried on a float trip, but stick to the dehydrated ones on goat and horse trips unless they will be served the first night.

Alpie, Sweet Pea, and Bob with their loads. Photo credit: Jeff Corney.

FIVE DAYS OF GOATPACKING MEALS

Harnessed to carts, goats have hauled necessities, luxuries, and humans for centuries. Yet utilizing them as true pack animals in the ways traditional to horses and mules only came about two decades ago. Since then, goatpacking has thrived as an alternative for people who love to trek through the backcountry, but don't enjoy carrying the heavy weight of backpacks.

Outfitted goatpacking excursions generally last from three to five days. While some full service (hired cook) trips exist, usually everybody does their own cooking. Following this rule of thumb, here are five days worth of menus and meals suitable for this type of animal-assisted trek.

Food for the trail

Since you'll be hiking alongside the goats and you'll carry trail food in your day pack, choose from the lunches listed below or from the lists given in the backpacking or horsepacking sections (pages 20, 120). Keep in mind your exertion level will be lower than when you backpack, therefore, plan for approximately 1/3 pound of trail food per person per day.

It's only fair to warn you. You may have to fend off a few goats over delectables such as peanut butter and jelly sandwiches, bagels, muffins, tortillas, and fresh fruit. After all, goats are just big kids who love PB and jelly sandwiches and crisp apples as much as we humans do.

I usually choose from the following:

peanut butter and jelly sandwiches
bagels filled with chopped chutney
refried beans (canned) spread on tortillas
summer sausage and rolls
assorted fresh fruit
tuna (canned) mixed with catchup on
    English muffins
muffins
assorted hard candies
shrimp (canned) with powdered onion and
    mustard on rye crackers
chocolate covered graham crackers
molasses cookies
oatmeal cookies

Supply list (5 days)

Baking Staples:
1–10 oz. container baking powder
1–16 oz. box baking soda

1 lb. blue cornmeal (can substitute yellow)
1 lb. brown sugar
1–8 oz. container cocoa
1–1 lb. box cornstarch
1–5 lb. sack white flour
1–5 lb. sack whole wheat flour
1 lb. jar honey
1–18 oz. container oats
1–1 lb. can powdered buttermilk
1–25.6 oz. box powdered milk
1–26 oz. box salt
1–5 lb. sack sugar

Bread Products:
1 pkg. English Muffins
1 pkg. tortillas

Canned Goods:
2–15 oz. can corned beef hash
1–2.25 oz. can sliced black olives
1–4 oz. can chopped green chiles
1–16 oz. sliced peaches in juice

Dried Fruit/Vegetables/Nuts:
1–2 oz. pkg. almond slivers
1 container candied fruits

Fresh Fruit:
1 cantaloupe
7 tomatoes
1 honeydew melon

Fresh Vegetables:
1 bell pepper

1 head cabbage
1 lb. bag carrots
1 bunch celery
1 eggplant
7 onions
1 purple onion
2 yellow squash

Frozen Food:
1–16 oz. pkg. frozen blueberries
1–10 oz. pkg. frozen green beans

Meat/Milk/Margarine/Cheese/Eggs:
2 lb. ground beef
1 1/2 lb. ground sausage
1/2 lb. ground turkey
1 lb. ham
1 lb. beef
1/4 lb. cheddar cheese
1–8 oz. container Parmesan cheese
6 eggs
1 1/2 lb. margarine
(optional canned milk, see recipes below)

Rice/Noodles:
1–16 oz. pkg. spinach noodles
1–16 oz. pkg. macaroni

Sauce & Other Mixes/Drinks/Speciality Items:
1–6 oz. box cornmeal stuffing mix
2–1.6 oz. pkg. Hollandaise Sauce Mix
1–.4 oz. pkg. ranch dressing mix
1–16 oz. box instant mashed potatoes
1 box Junket Rennet

1 lb. coffee
40 bags of assorted teas
1–10 oz. pkg. regular marshmallows

Spices:
1 container allspice
1 container caraway seeds
1 container cayenne pepper
1 container cinnamon
1 container ground coriander seed
1 container cumin
1 container garlic powder
1 container ginger
1 container mace
1 container nutmeg
1 container parsley flakes
1 container pepper
1 bottle vanilla

TRAIL LUNCHES: 1/3 lb. per person per day (see list above)

EXTRAS FOR THE TRAIL: A plastic bottle of soy sauce, Worcestershire sauce, honey, molasses, salt, and pepper.

DAY ONE

BREAKFAST

High Plains Hash
Coffee

TRAIL LUNCH

Shrimp (canned) with powdered onion and mustard
Rye crackers
Fresh fruit
Oatmeal cookies

DINNER

Tortillas des Carnes
Ensalada de Col
Melon
Tea

DAY ONE

No trails exist in much of Wyoming's two and a half million acres high plains Red Desert, other than those made by wild horses and antelope. Dry creek beds abound. Scattered bone fragments tell tales of hardship. And rising 500 feet out of this wasteland of sage and sand, the Honeycombs Buttes look carved by time's knife, exposing every color from deep magenta to olive green.

The March morning dawns with a mass of gun-metal gray clouds. John, our guide, keeps an eye on them as he fixes a broken strap on one of the pack saddles. Jeff stows gear in a set of panniers, the term for saddle bags used on pack animals. But I alone capture the attention of our seven curious pack goats because I'm fixing breakfast—High Plains Hash.

Back in the 1600s, "hash" described a wide variety of dishes made from leftover meat and vegetables. Settlers chopped the ingredients very fine, put them into a kettle of boiling water, added a bit of salt and pepper, and sprinkled enough dry flour over the mixture to produce a thick gravy. In the US Army of the 1700s and 1800s, the only difference between hash, stew, and soup was the amount of water used.

Day One Breakfast Recipe:

High Plains Hash

6 eggs
2–15 oz. can corned beef hash
6 English Muffins
2–1.6 oz. pkg. Hollandaise Sauce Mix

Wrap toilet paper around each egg and replace it in the carton. Tie the container closed. Pack remaining ingredients separately. Place eggs in the top of the pannier.

In the field preparation

After making coffee (see the recipe in the Backpack section on page 28), place a large pot on the stove, filled with cold water. Add eggs. Cover and bring to boil over high heat. Remove from stove and set aside. Open hash. Heat in saucepan. Meanwhile, collect large bowls. Place half of a muffin in the bottom. When hash is heated, spoon 1/8 of it into each bowl. Repeat with another two alternating layers of muffin and hash. Put lids on bowls to keep food warm while preparing sauce.

Blend 2 c. of cold water and the sauce mix. Heat over medium heat, stirring constantly until sauce thickens. Peel hard boiled eggs, reserving water for another round of hot drinks or washing up. Slice eggs. Arrange over the top layer of hash and muffins. Pour sauce over eggs and serve.

THIS MEAL requires no adaptation for use on horse-packing or float trips. It is only suitable on a backpack trip if you don't mind some extra weight caused by carrying canned hash and fresh eggs in a special plastic egg container (powdered eggs don't make an adequate substitute as they don't taste very good). As an option, the hash can be dehydrated. Allow for reconstituting time.

When it rains in the desert, the landscape turns to slick mud, almost impossible to trek through. Fortunately, the clouds dissipate by the time we pack up and head into what the locals simply call the "Honeycombs."

Since Jeff and I have asked John to show us the benefits of packing with goats, he immediately leads us up an almost perpendicular column of fifty million year old claystone that crumbles even as our fingers clutch for handholds. The goats dash past us like children playing tag on a level field. And they carry seventy pounds in their scaled-down pack saddles John designed and produces himself.

Resembling a sawbuck used on horses, John has modified the goat saddle so that it rides just behind the animal's shoulder blades and stops short of the hipbone. A rumpstrap and breast collar help keep saddle and cargo securely in place whether the goats amble straight up a column of claystone or trot down a steep gully.

The entire rig can be removed from a goat's back in a couple of minutes. As a demonstration, John stops next to Alpie, our lead goat and veteran of many pack trips. John removes the two five-gallon jugs of water from Alpie's panniers, unbuckles the cinch and two straps, then lifts saddle and blankets while the goat walks out from under it.

Jeff and I get in some practice by transferring the payload to Bob, a tenacious two year old. Still a teenager in goat years, Bob shouldn't haul this kind of weight for more than a few hours. When he begins to tire, we switch the water onto Menu's back.

Menu received that name because he was scheduled to be on the menu at a goat breeders conference until his owner attended a lecture John gave on goatpacking and thought Menu had the right temperament for it.

Menu reminds me of a family dog, lying down next to me when we stop for lunch on the sandy shore of an evaporated creek bed. I lean back against one of his panniers, using the brim of my hat to shade my eyes from the sun's relentless glare. He sighs and stretches his front legs out before him, half-dozing in the afternoon heat. His head sways slightly from side to side as the three of us talk. But the minute I rattle a plastic bag containing oatmeal cookies, he snaps his head around, cranes his neck forward, his lips begging for a morsel. Definitely reminiscent of "man's best friend."

After Menu receives his treat, I fix our lunch. Opening the can of tiny shrimp, I dump the contents into a plastic bag containing a bit of onion powder and mustard. Resealing the bag, I squeeze the contents until they are well mixed. Then I peel back the top so everybody can get to the filling to spread it on the rye crackers, not their hands.

Like us, goats can put in an eight to ten mile day in rough country. In the plains of the Red Desert, they can trek fifteen to twenty miles per day. Because goats can't sweat to keep cool, John refrains from traveling during the hottest part of the day or journeys by moonlight on summer desert trips. Fortunately for all of us, the constant breeze holds the sun's heat at bay on this springtime excursion.

When dusk approaches, we descend into a depression in the side of one of the buttes to get out of the ever-present wind.

Following rule number one when out with pack animals, we tend to them first. After we strip off the panniers and saddles, we stack the tack and place the blankets out to dry in what's left of the sunshine.

Next Jeff and I get to experience the most unique part of packing with goats—milking our doe Bonita. She provides us with a supply of fresh milk for drinking, cooking, and cheese on the journey.

John then hands us some alfalfa pellets, and all the goats gather around. Long-necked Sweet Pea captures more than his fair share. In all the jostling, many of the cubes land on the ground. Not to worry. Unlike grain that scatters rather than gets consumed, Newlio steps in and gobbles them right up, leaving nothing behind.

Later the goats disburse around the campsite and munch on some greasewood. Of all the pack animals available today (including llamas), goats impact fragile environments the least. Instead of mowing native grasses, they nibble a bit of sagebrush here, crunch a few pine needles or willows there, or nip at some bitterbrush. Just like people, mealtime variety makes goats happy campers.

Then it's time to light the stove and begin preparing our dinner, Tortillas des Carnes. Mexican foods go great with hot weather. By the end of the Mexican War in 1848, south-of-the-border cuisine had become a popular and welcome addition to the American diet. Meat was generally prepared with the liberal amounts of either red or green chiles that had been blistered and peeled before mixing them with the meat. Cooks accomplished this by holding the peppers one at a time over the flames of an open fire pit until the pepper's skin charred and bubbled. Once brown, the peppers were placed, still hot, in a covered jar and allowed to sweat until they cooled enough to handle. This made it easier to peel off the skins. Finally the chiles were ready to use.

John feeding the goats. Photo credit: Jeff Corney.

Day One Dinner Recipes:

Tortillas des Carnes
1 lb. beef, sliced
8 tortillas
1 onion
1–2.25 oz. can sliced black olives
1–4 oz. can chopped green chiles
1 t. cumin
1 T. margarine
    Sprinkle cumin on beef slices. Freeze in a zipper bag. Also freeze tortillas. Pack remaining ingredients for trip, storing onion in a net bag and keeping margarine separate. When ready to leave on the trip, bag both frozen items together and keep in an ice chest until packing them in the panniers.

Ensalada de Col
1/3 head of cabbage
1 small purple onion
1 bell pepper
1–.4 oz. pkg. ranch dressing mix
4 T. powdered buttermilk
1/2 c. goat milk
    Place the cabbage section and bell pepper in a vegetable zipper bag. Store onion in the net bag. Mix and bag together dressing mix and buttermilk powder. The goat milk will be obtained in the field. If no producing doe is scheduled for your trip, substitute 1/4 c. powdered milk and blend with dressing mixture before bagging. Keep fresh vegetables in an ice chest until ready to pack in the panniers at the roadhead.

Melon
1 honeydew melon
    Pack whole for the trip.

In the field preparation

Melt margarine in the skillet. Chop onion. Stir fry meat and onion in the margarine over medium heat until cooked. Lay tortillas on the lid while meat cooks in order to heat them. Open olives and green chiles, draining each. Add them to the meat mixture, stirring until well mixed. Cover and remove from heat.

Collect large bowls and put on a pot of water for tea and doing dishes.

Shred cabbage and place in large pot. Chop bell pepper and onion. Add goat milk to bag of dressing mixture. Reseal and gently squeeze until blended. Pour over cabbage. Mix well. Serve in bowls. Serve meat mixture rolled up in warm tortillas.

Slice melon and serve. Give pepper and melon seeds and rind to the goats.

THIS MEAL requires no adaptation for horsepacking or float trips. For backpacking, dehydrate meat, onion, and canned vegetables used in the Tortillas des Carnes and the fresh vegetables used in the Ensalada de Col. Substitute 4 T. powdered milk and 1/2 c. water for the fresh in accordance with the recipe. Fresh honeydew can be carried if you don't mind the extra weight. Otherwise select a lighter backpacking dessert as the flavor washes out of honeydew when it's been dried, then reconstituted.

Once we finish dinner, John extracts a button squeeze box, a small accordion-like instrument, from one of the panniers and plays a polka. The goats cluster around us, listening and falling asleep one by one as the polka drifts into a waltz.

Unlike horses, goats don't require fencing, hobbling, or highline tying to keep them near camp overnight. They enjoy people company. In fact, Menu beds down in the vestibule of our tent, staying there through much of the night.

DAY TWO

BREAKFAST

Cantaloupe Crepes
Coffee

TRAIL LUNCH

Peanut butter and jelly sandwiches
Chocolate covered graham crackers
Fresh fruit

DINNER

Army Life Stew
Whole Wheat Biscuits
Goat Milk Custard
Tea

DAY TWO

Next morning, we breakfast on Cantaloupe Crepes. A member of the muskmelon family, this fruit has been cultivated in America since colonial days. People ate it raw— sliced or combined with other in-season fruits for breakfast or with ice cream for dessert. However, industrious jelly makers turned the melon into Cantaloupe Conserve, a type of jam, and served it with bread.

Day Two Breakfast Recipe:

Cantaloupe Crepes
1 cantaloupe
1 c. flour
1/4 c. sugar
1/2 t. salt
1/4 t. coriander
5 T. margarine
1/4 c. sugar
1 t. cinnamon
1/4 t. mace
goat milk

Pack cantaloupe whole for the trip. Mix next four ingredients together and bag. Mix sugar and spices together and store in separate bag from the margarine. If no milking doe will accompany you, substitute 1/4 c. powdered milk for the fresh and bag it in with flour mixture.

In the field preparation

Chop cantaloupe, giving seeds and rind to the goats while the water is boiling for coffee. Add 1 c. of water to flour mixture, making a thin batter. Melt a bit of margarine in skillet to lightly grease it. Spoon about 2 T. of batter into the skillet, tilting it to spread batter. Flip when crepe browns on the bottom and bubbles on top, cooking the other side. Repeat until all batter is used. Sprinkle cinnamon sugar mix over the top of each crepe. Spoon on some canteloupe and serve. Makes 7–8 crepes.

THIS MEAL needs no adaptation on horsepacking and float trips. For backpacking, dehydrate the melon, then reconstitute it when ready to fix breakfast.

When we break camp, we inspect the site for telltale signs of our presence. There are none. Goats tread virtually unnoticed in the wilderness because the tracks and droppings they leave behind blend in with those of deer, antelope, or bighorn sheep.

Normally one goat hauls all supplies for one person. We brought more in order to cache water for John's summer excursions into the desert. Plus, two rookies came along, sporting extra light loads so they could "learn the ropes."

Like their human counterparts, kids master packing by watching the grown-ups. Actual training begins as early as two weeks to a month old. John brings the youngsters along with mom as soon as they are able to keep up with the herd. This way they accept traveling in rainy weather and getting their feet wet, literally.

Goats tend to shy away from water and leap over streams whenever possible. But when the kids (the goat kind) see the adults crossing wider creeks without complaint, they follow suit.

As the kids grow, John introduces them to pack saddles by fashioning a cinch strap from a soft belt covered with thick layers of burlap. He wraps it around the kid's middle. Once they accept it, John attaches a blanket to the strap. By the time they reach five or six months, they wear a mini version of a saddle with short panniers. At a year old, bucks can pack about thirty pounds.

An adult wether (neutered buck) can carry close to one third of his body weight, or about seventy to seventy-five pounds. Does can haul between twenty-five and thirty pounds. Of course, they also furnish milk!

Once we make camp and milk Bonita, I begin dinner. The Whole Wheat Biscuits require baking; however in the desert, twigs can be a rare commodity. So instead of using a lid fire, I pat the biscuits quite flat and cook them like pancakes over the stove's lowest heat, flipping them to "bake" one side at a time. Then I fix the Army Life Stew.

While beef never replaced pork as the main meat rationed to American soldiers during the eighteenth and nineteenth centuries, when supplies were available, each enlisted man received one and one-quarter pound of either fresh or salt beef per day. And the Army regulated how the meat could be cooked! The beef was cubed and simmered in a pot of water for precisely one and one-half hours. Any vegetables in season (many forts had gardens to supplement vegetable rations which usually consisted of beans or peas), potatoes, if available, and salt were added. The brew was simmered about two hours until the meat became tender.

Day Two Dinner Recipes:

Army Life Stew
1 lb. ground beef
1/2 lb. ground turkey
6 carrots
6 stalks celery
2 onions
2 c. macaroni
2 T. parsley flakes
1 t. nutmeg

1 t. cayenne

1/2 c. Parmesan cheese

Brown beef and turkey together. Freeze in a zipper bag with parsley, nutmeg, pepper, and cheese. Store carrots and celery in vegetable zipper bag. Put onion in net bag. Bag macaroni separately. (If you will be traveling in a hot climate, dehydrate the beef and turkey after browning.)

Whole Wheat Biscuits

1 2/3 c. whole wheat flour

1/3 c. flour

4 T. powdered buttermilk

1 t. salt

1 t. baking powder

1 t. baking soda

3 T. margarine

Blend and bag all ingredients except margarine.

Goat Milk Custard

3 c. goat milk

4 T. sugar

2 T. vanilla

1 1/2 tablets Junket Rennet

1/3 c. honey

1 t. coriander

1 t. allspice

Mix honey with coriander and allspice. Store in a small plastic bottle. Also store vanilla in plastic bottle. Bag sugar and rennet tablet separately. Goat milk will be obtained in the field. If you aren't packing with a producing doe, substitute 1/2 c. powdered milk and 3 c. water. NOTE: canned milk cannot be substituted for fresh or powdered as it won't react to the rennet well enough to create a firm custard.

In the field preparation

Chop carrots, celery, and onion. Place all stew ingredients in the large pot. Cover and bring to a boil over high heat in enough water to cover mixture. Boil for 5 minutes, then remove from heat and wrap in a piece of ensolite to keep stew warm. Collect large and small bowls.

While water for tea is heating, cut margarine into biscuit mix. Add 1 1/4 c. of cold water to dry ingredients or enough to form a soft dough. Pat into biscuits about 1/2 inch thick. Bake in the skillet with a lid fire 10–12 minutes until browned. Makes 12–14.

Return stew to the stove and simmer 15–20 minutes or until vegetables are tender. Serve with biscuits.

When ready for dessert, combine milk, sugar, and vanilla in smaller pot. Heat over low fire until lukewarm (just barely warm to the touch when you dip your finger in milk). Meanwhile, dissolve rennet in 2 T. cold water. When milk is warm, add rennet, stirring vigorously for three seconds only. Pour mixture into bowls and set aside. Leave undistributed for 15 minutes. Heat honey and spices in smaller pot (don't need to clean out first) until warm. Pour over pudding and serve.

THIS MEAL needs no adaptations for horsepacking or float trips. For backpacking, dehydrate all the meat and vegetables in the stew recipe. Substitute powdered milk for fresh in the custard.

DAY THREE

BREAKFAST

Blue Cornmeal Mush
Coffee

TRAIL LUNCH

Bagels with chopped chutney
Fresh fruit
Assorted hard candies

DINNER

Eggplant Bonita
Desert Blueberry Pie
Tea

DAY THREE

For breakfast, I prepare Blue Cornmeal Mush. Blue corn, native to New Mexico, adds an earthy flavor to the traditional version of what settlers called "stirabout," "porridge," and even "hasty pudding." Pilgrims learned how to fix this simple dish from the Indians. They threw handfuls of cornmeal into a pot of boiling water, added a bit of salt, and cooked it about half an hour, stirring constantly to keep lumps from forming. One frontier cook claimed mush and Johnny Cake (cornbread) were all human beings needed to start the day.

Day Three Breakfast Recipe:

Blue Cornmeal Mush
1 1/4 c. blue cornmeal
1 t. salt
3 T. sugar
3 T. powdered milk
Mix all ingredients and bag.

In the field preparation

After heating water for coffee, stir cornmeal mix into 4 c. of cold water that has been poured into the large pot. Cover. Bring to boil over medium heat. Reduce to low and cook 5 minutes, stirring constantly.

THIS MEAL requires no adaptation for any of the other trips.

We stop at an ant hill about a foot in diameter. Ever the curious one, Julio sniffs it. John scoops a handful of sand and rock chips the ants have mounded, letting it trickle through his fingers as he checks for flakes. Flakes refer to micro slivers broken off of stones as Native Americans fashioned them into tools or arrowheads. Lots of flakes on an ant hill suggests an Indian camping ground some place in the vicinity.

Archaeologists have discovered pit houses dating back 6,500 years in the Red Desert. The hunter-gatherer cultures of prehistoric and historic Indians flourished in what looks like absolute desolation to the untrained eye. They harvested the rice grass we walk through and the biscuit root. Plains Indians actually used the latter as trail food. Beside eating the roots raw (they taste like a cross between a sweet potato and a turnip), the Indians dried the roots and ground them into a flour. Afterward, they baked the bread, known as *cous,* in the shape of a doughnut, strung them through a thong of leather and hung them from the horse—the equivalent of trail bagels.

Our bagels aren't so exotic, but we find them just as tasty, spreading fruity chutney on the halves for a satisfying lunch.

Caverns, like those John caches water in, abound in the Honeycombs. We take full advantage of one when lightning hits nearby. It's close enough that it buzzed in Jeff's ears, so we scramble into the cave and wait for the storm to pass.

Inside we find a stash of driftwood, caught and held among the mudstone formation. This means I can bake a blueberry pie tonight instead of having to convert the recipe into blueberry pancakes.

Early colonists found many berries that looked familiar to them, especially blueberries. However, they mistook them for the English bilberry. Cooks preserved berries by boiling them in some sugar until the ingredients turned into a thick syrup. Then they spread the fruit on pieces of paper and laid them in the sun to dry. Once dehydrated, these forerunners to what we call "fruit leather" were rolled up and stored in a dry place. When the family wanted blueberry pie, the cook pealed off enough berry filling from the paper and dropped it in a pan of boiling water and sugar until reconstituted.

Day Three Dinner Recipes:

Eggplant Bonita
1/2 lb. sausage
1 eggplant, chopped
4 tomatoes, chopped
1 onion, diced
4 stalks celery, chopped
1/3 c. margarine
1–6 oz. box cornmeal stuffing mix
Brown sausage before dehydrating. Dry eggplant, tomatoes, onion, and celery. Bag sausage and onion together (or onion can be taken fresh into the field). Bag remaining vegetables with the seasoning packet that comes with the stuffing mix. Store stuffing bread and margarine separately.

Desert Blueberry Pie
1–16 oz. pkg. frozen blueberries
1/2 c. sugar
1/2 t. mace
1 T. cornstarch
1 recipe Trailblazer Biscuit mix (see Index)
Dehydrate blueberries and bag. Mix sugar and mace. Store separately from cornstarch. Bag Trailblazer Biscuit mix separately.

In the field preparation
Rehydrate meat and vegetables. Make hot drinks. Bring sausage, vegetables, stuffing seasoning, 1/3 c. margarine, and 1 1/2 c. water to a boil in the large pot. Cover and boil 5 minutes. Add stuffing bread. Remove from heat. Let it sit, covered, a few minutes, then serve.

Reconstitute blueberries on the lid of the eggplant. Prepare biscuit mix according to the recipe, but instead of forming biscuits, spread in skillet, and bake with a lid fire for 40–45 minutes.

After the biscuit dough is cooked and blueberries are completely rehydrated, bring blueberries and sugar mixture to boil in 1 c. water. Mix cornstarch with 1 T. water in small bowl. When blueberries are boiling, add cornstarch mixture and boil 1 minute, stirring constantly. Remove from heat. Scoop out the center of the biscuit, reserving bread. Be sure to leave at least a 1/2 inch of bread in the bottom of the skillet. Pour blueberries into the center. Crumble bread on top. Serve.

AS AN OPTION on float trips, take frozen sausage and fresh vegetables and fresh, canned, or frozen blueberries in an ice chest. For backpacking and horsepacking trips, no adaptation is needed, unless you want to substitute canned blueberry pie filling for fruit, sugar, and cornstarch.

SPECIAL: Goat Camp Cheese (start tonight for tomorrow, see recipe on page 108).

DAY FOUR

BREAKFAST

Buttermilk Oatmeal Biscuits
Goat Camp Cheese
Dried Fruit
Coffee

TRAIL LUNCH

Refried beans (canned) spread on tortillas
Fresh fruit
Molasses cookies

DINNER

Goat Flats Grub
Glacier Ice Cream
(or Iceless Cream)
Tea

DAY FOUR

Cheese has been around for 4,000 years—the result of a happy accident of a long-ago desert traveler. An Arab merchant stored a supply of milk in a bag made out of a sheep's stomach. Rennet, a natural part of the animal's stomach lining, caused curds to form in a watery substance called whey. At the end of the day when he sat down to drink his milk, he found cheese. It satisfied his hunger and the whey eased his thirst.

Pioneer cooks made rennet by cleaning out a calf's stomach, being sure to leave any pieces of curd (the last milk eaten by the calf) inside. They next soaked the stomach in a quart of water and hung it to dry. The liquid was bottled and used a spoonful or two at a time to make cheese.

Day Four Breakfast Recipes:

Buttermilk Oatmeal Biscuits

3/4 c. oats
1 c. flour
2 T. powdered buttermilk
3 T. sugar
1/2 t. nutmeg
1 t. baking powder
1/2 t. baking soda
1 t. salt
2 T. margarine
　　Mix and bag all ingredients except margarine.

Goat Camp Cheese

4 c. goat milk
1/2 tablet Junket Rennet
1 t. salt
　　Pack rennet tablet and a shaker of salt. If no producing

doe will accompany you on the journey, take along an extra 1/2 lb. of cheddar cheese. NOTE: powdered or canned milk will not react to rennet and let curds form.

In the field preparation

Dissolve rennet in 1/4 c. cold water. Set aside. Heat milk in the smaller pot over a low fire until *just barely warm to the touch*. No steam should be rising from the milk. If it gets too warm (lukewarm is too warm), remove from heat and cool. When the temperature of the milk is correct, remove from the stove and add rennet solution, stirring well. Cover with a wool shirt or sweater. Leave undisturbed overnight.

In the morning after fixing coffee, put cold water in the large pot. Nest the pot containing the cheese on top of the larger pot. Cut curd in large squares (1 inch). Light stove. Cook curds, uncovered, over lowest possible heat for 30 minutes. Do not stir for the first 15 minutes. Then stir gently (one counterclockwise circle with the spoon) once every five minutes for the last 15 minutes. Remove from stove. Cover and set aside while preparing biscuit dough.

Melt margarine in the skillet. Pour it and enough cold water into dry ingredients to make a sticky dough. Form biscuits, patting to about 1/2 inch thick. Bake in the skillet over low heat and a lid fire about 10–12 minutes. Makes 17–18.

Drain whey from the cheese, reserving it for a unique drink. Add salt, stir gently, and set aside. Serve cheese over biscuits, or as an option, with honey and dried fruit.

THIS MEAL requires no adaptation (other than substituting cheddar for camp cheese) for any of the other kinds of trips.

On the trail, John points to an established antelope path that leads to a spring. Hoof prints left by the herd match those of the goats.

These two species share common ancestors. From the goat-antelope genes come a greater tolerance to heat, smoother running and walking gate, and better awareness. French Alpines such as Alpie and the Oberhasli like Bob tolerate heat better than other breeds. Saanens like Julio and Sweet Pea, as well as Saanen-Toggenburg crossbreeds like Newlio and Bonita, have endurance, calm dispositions, and tend to grow larger than other breeds. Then LaManchas such as Menu are the most docile breed.

Cross-breeding to obtain these desirable traits, John produces pack goats adapted to cold or warm weather conditions, as well as high altitudes. Another advantage of these breeds is their agility when it comes to traveling in high mountain terrain. Goats have a better instinct for traversing snowfields than other pack animals. They test the snow first, and if it sounds hollow, they won't proceed. And unlike we humans, they can walk in as much as three feet of snow without getting bogged down.

Of course, the real reward for snow travel with pack goats comes in the form of ice cream. Lucky travelers on the Oregon Trail discovered the Ice Slough, a natural phenomenon on the route, where ice could always be found—even in the height of summer. Therefore, many pioneers celebrated the Fourth of July with fresh ice cream. Charles Parke, one emigrant to the Far West, wrote down his recipe for *Ice Cream at the South Pass of the Rockies.* He put two quarts of milk in a tin bucket and sweetened it with sugar and peppermint. This bucket went into a wooden bucket, and he packed alternate layers of snow and salt around the tin container. With the aid of a clean stick, he stirred the mixture until it transformed into ice cream so delicious that the whole company decided to fire a salute outside his tent in appreciation, "bursting one gun but injuring no one."

Day Four Dinner Recipes:

Goat Flats Grub

1 lb. ground beef
2 yellow squash, sliced thin
1 onion, chopped
1 t. pepper
1 t. garlic powder
3 c. spinach noodles
1/4 c. Parmesan cheese

Brown ground beef. Dry meat, squash, and onion. Bag with pepper and garlic powder. Store noodles and cheese in two separate bags.

Glacier Ice Cream

1 large pot snow
goat milk
1/4 c. sugar
2 T. cocoa

Bag sugar and cocoa together. If you won't have a producing doe along, substitute canned or powdered milk.

In the field preparation

Reconstitute meat mixture while heating water for hot drinks. In a covered, large pot, bring meat mixture and 2 c. of cold water to a boil. Reduce heat to medium. Cook until food is tender. Add enough water to bring level back up to 2 c. and when mixture is boiling, toss in noodles. Cook until noodles are done and most of the liquid is absorbed. Divide into large bowls. Sprinkle with cheese. Serve.

For dessert, fill a large pot with fresh snow. Sprinkle sugar mixture on it. Stir in enough fresh goat milk to create the consistency of ice cream. Serve.

AS AN OPTION on float trips, freeze meat and take fresh

vegetables. Substitute Iceless Cream (see below). Otherwise, this meal can be carried as is on horsepacking and backpacking trips.

Since we aren't anywhere near snow or the Ice Slough tonight, I make Iceless Cream instead.

Iceless Cream
1–10 oz. pkg. regular marshmallows
3 c. crispy rice cereal
1/4 c. cocoa
goat milk
2 T. margarine
Bag everything separately. If not taking a producing doe, substitute either canned or powdered milk.

In the field preparation
Melt margarine in smaller pot over low heat. Add marshmallows, stirring constantly until melted. Add cocoa, stirring until well blended. Blend in cereal, then enough milk to make mixture slushy. Serve.

DAY FIVE

BREAKFAST

Julio Potato Ham Melt
Coffee

TRAIL LUNCH

Tuna (canned) with catsup on English muffins
Assorted fresh fruit
Molasses cookies

DINNER

Sweet Pea's Peachy Favorite
Menu's Treat Teacake
Tea

DAY FIVE

Into the nineteenth century, people persisted in viewing both potatoes and tomatoes as poisonous. Cookbooks warned that each should only be eaten if well cooked. Potatoes were boiled to get rid of the "toxins." People threw out the cooking water, which absorbed the poison they thought caused leprosy. Likewise, the only safe way to eat tomatoes involved cooking them at least three hours to remove the "raw taste." Many settlers believed raw tomatoes caused cancer.

Day Five Breakfast Recipe:

Julio Potato Ham Melt
4 slices ham, ground
3 tomatoes, chopped
2 1/4 c. instant mashed potatoes
1 t. salt
1 t. pepper
1 T. parsley flakes
1/4 lb. cheese, chopped
3 T. margarine
goat milk

Dehydrate ham and tomatoes. Bag together. Bag instant potatoes separately from remaining ingredients. As always, keep margarine separate. Substitute 1/4 c. powdered milk if not taking a producing doe.

In the field preparation

Rehydrate ham and tomatoes while boiling water for coffee. Bring a large pot containing ham mixture and an additional 3 1/4 c. water to a boil. Simmer until ham mixture is tender. Add milk, seasonings, and instant potatoes. Remove from heat. Stir in cheese. Serve.

AS AN OPTION on float trips, take frozen ham and fresh

tomatoes. Otherwise, this meal needs no adaptation for the other trips.

Early in 1972, the US Forest Service hired John to study a herd of bighorn sheep. He needed a way to transport gear and sensitive scientific equipment into the high country. He'd packed with horses for many years and had a couple of goats trained to pull a cart. Horses, however, couldn't cross boulder fields or climb glaciers to keep up with the bighorns. Goats could.

Sure-footed relatives of the sheep family, goats feel as much at home on the mountain peaks of the bighorns' habitat as they do in the barnyard. Furthermore, they made it possible for John to keep a close eye on his subjects as a goat's eyesight is seven times greater than a human's. When one of his goats stopped and stared at something in the distance, he would put a pair of binoculars between the goat's horns and get a fix on sheep he would have otherwise missed.

Goats also pick their path rather than barging through underbrush or low tree limbs. Handy when carrying things such as microscopes or wine goblets (depending on the occasion) in the panniers.

On this trip, we didn't bring fancy crystal or equipment. Instead I pull canned peaches out of the panniers—something more rare than crystal until late in the 1800s. Women literally canned peached by filling tin cans with peeled, sliced fruit. They poured a syrup made from boiling a pint of sugar in a quart of water for five minutes over the peaches, then soldered the covers on the cans. Using a nail, the cooks pierced a small hole in the top to let steam escape, and put the cans in a washtub filled with water to just below the tops of the cans. This boiled for five minutes over an open fire, then the cans were removed and sealed with more solder.

Day Five Dinner Recipes:

Sweet Pea's Peachy Favorite
1 lb. ground sausage
2 onions, chopped
1–10 oz. pkg. frozen green beans (or 1 lb. fresh), cut
1 t. coriander
1 t. cumin
2 t. cinnamon
1 t. ginger
1–16 oz. can sliced peaches in juice
1/3 c. almond slivers
    Brown sausage. Dehydrate meat, onion, and beans. Bag dry foods with spices. Store almonds separately. Pack the canned peaches.

Menu's Treat Teacake
1 2/3 c. flour
1 c. brown sugar, firmly packed
1 t. caraway seeds
1 t. cinnamon
1/2 c. candied fruits
1/2 c. margarine
goat milk
    Bag first five ingredients together. Store fruit and margarine separately. If there will be no producing doe on the trip, substitute 1/3 c. powdered milk.

In the field preparation
    Rehydrate meat mixture. Cover. Bring to a boil in the large pot. Open peaches. Add them to meat, juice and all. Simmer until tender, adding more water as needed to maintain about 2 inches of water in the bottom of the pot. Stir frequently. Add almonds and serve.

While eating dinner, melt margarine in the skillet. In a pot, blend flour mixture with candied fruits. Add margarine and enough water to make a stiff dough. Spread in skillet. Cover and bake with a lid fire for 40–50 minutes. Serve with milk or hot tea.

AS AN OPTION on float trips, substitute frozen sausage, frozen, fresh or canned beans, and fresh onion. This meal is suitable for backpacking by dehydrating the peaches and for horsepacking as is. Canned beans and peaches can be taken if you don't mind the extra weight.

Horsepacking in the Rockies. Photo credit: Jeff Corney.

SEVEN DAYS OF HORSEPACKING MEALS

The tradition of horsepacking in the American West dates back to not long after Plains Indians captured the first wild horses. Like these tribes, explorers, mountain men, and miners adopted horsepacking as a way of life. Nowadays, outfitters continue the practice of this ancient custom.

Horsepacking excursions come in many forms. Guest ranches often include horsepacking treks as part of the vacation package. These last anywhere from overnight to several days in the field. Then there's completely outfitted expeditions which the whole family, including very small children, can enjoy together.

Most outfitters provide full service horse trips with hired cooks and wranglers who care for the animals in the field and do all the loading, unloading, setting up and breaking down of camp. Some outfitters, however, do offer hands-on trips for do-it-yourselfers. Both of these types of horsepacking ventures can last a week or more. Therefore, here are seven days worth of meals suitable for horsepacking adventures.

Food on the trail

Horsepacking provides days of perpetual motion. It isn't fair to horses or mules loaded down with 100 to 150 pounds to stand around while humans stop for lunch, so you'll usually consume trail foods while riding rather than taking breaks. Think of your saddlebags as lunch boxes on horseback. They protect the food and keep it readily accessible.

Bagels, sandwiches with cheese and hard salami or summer sausage, fresh fruit, candy or granola bars all work well for horse-borne mid-day meals. Or choose from the list of sandwich fillers below.

As with goatpacking, keep in mind the horse hauls the weight, therefore a standard workday or school day lunch like a bagel, some salami, cheese, and a piece of fruit will adequately satisfy the appetite. Horsepacking lunches fall closer to one-quarter pound per person per day.

Sandwich fillers

Cheddar cheese grated with chopped sweet
pickle, and chili sauce
Saddle Bags Chicken Spread (see recipe below)
Cold Cuts with Chinese Hot Mustard
Corned beef hash and horseradish
Crab Pardner (see recipe below)
Dates chopped with almonds
Deviled ham and chopped dill pickles

Hard Salami with sliced Cheddar and horseradish
Peanut butter and chopped prunes
Peanut butter with banana chips
Sardine Sling (see recipe below)
Parmesan Half Hitch (see recipe below)
Hot Carrot Spread (see recipe below)

EXTRAS FOR THE TRAIL: A plastic bottle of soy sauce, Worcestershire sauce, honey, molasses, salt, and pepper.

Supply list (7 days)

Baking Staples:
1–10 oz. box baking powder
1 lb. brown sugar
1 lb. buckwheat flour
1–16 oz. box cornstarch
1–25.6 oz. box powdered milk
1–16 oz. can powdered buttermilk
1–26 oz. box salt
1–5 lb. sack flour
1–18 oz. box oats
1–5 lb. sack sugar
1 lb. whole wheat flour

Canned Goods:
1–16 oz. can apricots in juice
1–14 oz. can bean sprouts
1–5 oz. can chicken
1–6 oz. can crab meat
2–10 3/4 oz. cans cream of asparagus soup
1–10 1/2 oz. cans cream of mushroom soup
2–16 oz. cans fruit cocktail in juice
2–15 1/2 oz. cans kidney beans

1–11 oz. can Mandarin Orange segments
1–16 oz. can sliced peaches in juice
1–20 oz. can pineapple chunks in juice
2–14 3/4 oz. cans salmon
1–7 oz. can Salsa Verde
2–3.75 oz. cans sardines in mustard

Crackers/Cereals/Breads:
1–15 oz. box crisp rice cereal
1 lb. box graham crackers
2 large flour tortillas
1–10 oz. bag pretzels
1 lb. box saltine crackers
1 loaf sliced bread
8 whole wheat flour tortillas

Dried Fruit/Vegetables/Nuts:
1 c. mixed dried fruit
1/4 c. nuts
1/3 c. pecans
1–1 lb. box raisins

Fresh Fruit:
2 apples
1 cantaloupe
1 watermelon

Fresh Vegetables:
3 bell peppers
3 carrots
2 cloves garlic
2 eggplants
1 head cabbage
22 mushrooms

6 onions
5 potatoes
1 bunch celery
6 tomatoes

Frozen Food:
1–16 oz. pkg. frozen broccoli
1–16 oz. pkg frozen corn
1–10 oz. pkg. frozen corn
1–16 oz. pkg. frozen peas
1–16 oz. pkg. frozen peas and carrots

Meat/Milk/Margarine/Cheese/Eggs:
16 eggs
1 lb. bag egg noddles
1–8 oz. container Parmesan cheese
1/2 lb. cheese
1/2 lb. Swiss cheese
1 lb. summer sausage
5 chicken franks
1–4.5 oz. jar dried beef
2 lbs. ground beef
2 lbs. sausage
1 lb. margarine

Rice/Noodles:
1–16 oz. bag spinach noodles

Sauce & Other Mixes/Drinks/Speciality Items:
1–20 oz. can hot chocolate mix
1–14 oz. bag caramels
1 bottle catsup
1 plastic jar chunky peanut butter
1–8 oz. container cocoa

1–2.9 oz. box custard mix
1 bottle honey
1 jar horseradish
1 jar Hot English Mustard
1 bottle reconstituted lemon juice
1 jar mayonnaise
1 bottle molasses
1 bottle soy sauce
1 bottle Tabasco
1 bottle vinegar
1–1.5 oz. pkg. white sauce mix
1 bottle Worcestershire sauce
assorted flavors of fruit crystals
60 assorted tea bags and coffee (optional)

Spices:
1 container allspice
1 container basil
1 container caraway seed
1 container cayenne pepper
1 container chili powder
1 container cinnamon
1 container dry mustard
1 container garlic powder
1 container hickory smoke salt
1 container nutmeg
1 container onion powder
1 container paprika
1 container parsley flakes
1 container pepper

LUNCHES: Choose from the list in Sandwich Fillers, spread on bagels, bread, rolls, tortillas, or muffins. Also take along fresh fruit for on the trail. (About 1/4 pound per person per day.)

DAY ONE

BREAKFAST

Irish Canyon Eggs
Coffee

TRAIL LUNCH

Cheddar cheese grated with chopped sweet pickle,
Chili sauce
Saddle Bags Chicken Spread
Fresh fruit

DINNER

Mule Meatloaf
Rumpstrap
Panniers Pecan Delight
Tea

DAY ONE

Frost glitters in the mid-June sunshine as we unload horses and gear at the Irish Canyon roadhead in Wyoming's Wind River Range. The two horses and one mule we'll be packing with on this trip belong to Teri. She invited us to bring our horses and join her on a test run for Smoke, Blaze, and Sandy the mule, the latest additions to the herd Teri started for her outfitting business.

Kirk and Joy, Teri's brother and sister-in-law, take a matched pair of chestnuts named Dancer and Prancer out of the trailer. Alex leads his paint, nicknamed Pain (short for Pain-in-the-Neck), to a line of pines at the edge of the parking lot and ties Pain to a tree trunk near the other horses while I unload Onyx.

Although Teri asked me to coordinate the rations on this informal trip, we'll take turns cooking. So once we grain the horses and mule, the others make sandwiches and pack the lunches in our saddle bags while I prepare a roadhead breakfast of Irish Canyon Eggs.

In spring, the Cheyenne gathered large quantities of wild fowl eggs to supplement their diet. When white settlers crossed these mountains, heading for the West Coast, some brought preserved eggs with them. The pioneers greased the shells of raw eggs with melted mutton or pork fat, then packed them tightly in a box filled with bran, straw, or ashes. Eggs, thus saved, lasted up to three months.

Day One Breakfast Recipe:

Irish Canyon Eggs
10 mushrooms, sliced thin
1/2 onion, diced
1–14 oz. can bean sprouts
6 eggs

2 T. powdered milk

1 t. salt

1/2 t. cayenne pepper

Dehydrate mushrooms and onion. Bag them with the powdered milk, salt, and pepper.

In the field preparation

Rehydrate mushroom and onion by pouring the can of bean sprouts into them. Reseal and set aside. Make coffee. Pour mushroom mixture into the skillet. Cover. Bring to boil over medium heat. Beat eggs and add to mushroom mixture. Scramble over medium heat until done.

THIS MEAL needs no adaptation for float or goat trips. For backpacking this is only suitable for a first day meal, provided you don't mind the extra weight caused by the eggs and canned goods. (Powdered eggs just don't taste good enough to be an adequate substitute.)

Day One Lunch Recipe:

Saddle Bag Chicken Spread

1–5 oz. can chicken

1/3 c. pecans, chopped

2 T. honey

1 T. lemon juice

Pack each item separately.

In the field preparation

Open chicken. Pour into the bag of nuts. Add remaining ingredients. Reseal bag and squeeze gently to mix. Spread on bread, bagels, or muffins.

THIS LUNCH is suitable for goat and float trips.

Back in 1859 Randolph Marcy wrote in his book, *The Prairie Traveler,* "it is no uncommon thing for them [cruel masters] to load their mules with the enormous burden of three or four hundred pounds." Nowadays, accepted carrying capacity ranges between ten and fifteen percent of the animal's total body weight, which translates into 100 to 150 pounds. Therefore panniers (saddle bags for pack animals) should weigh in the neighborhood of sixty pounds each, which allows for a top load in the form of a sack of grain, hay pellets, or sleeping bags. And don't forget you have to heft those panniers up onto the pack saddle riding high on a tall horse!

Teri uses a sawbuck, a popular style of pack saddle that can trace its origins back to a Native American design. Where Indians utilized the forks of a deer or elk's antlers, modern sawbucks have wooden front and back cross-pieces in the shape of an "X" that the panniers hang from.

Unless you're hauling a bunch of extras such as wall tents, cots, or even portable bathtubs, one horse (or mule) can carry all the gear for two people. Since we have three pack animals and only five people, there's room for a two-burner stove, a folding table for the camp kitchen, cast iron dutch oven, and battery operated lanterns (all plastic except for the lightbulbs).

Carrying food on horsepacking trips requires some special wrapping and packing to keep thing from rattling inside the panniers and spooking the pack animal. I double bag every recipe. Margarine goes in a plastic container with a screw on lid, and that gets put in a zipper bag. (Ruptured margarine containers make a greasy mess.) Old-timers used to store eggs in their flour sacks or pancake mix. I prefer wrapping each egg in toilet paper, replacing it in the carton, then tying the carton closed. The eggs go on top of everything else in the pannier. Right under the eggs, I pack the first night's dinner ingredients so I won't have to dig for them when it comes time to eat.

All non-perishable foods for each meal get packed into a cardboard box, stuffed with enough newspapers to keep items from shifting when you shake the box, then taped shut and labeled. I also mark on the outside of the box the amounts and types of perishable food that go with this meal.

Unless you view kerosene or stove gas as that special ingredient that adds zest to your meals, don't pack them in the same panniers with the food. Of course, if you're only packing with one horse, place the fuel bottles in the bottom of the pannier toward the back end (the horse's, that is). If the horse crashes into a tree and the fuel bottles happen to be in the front of the pannier, they could rupture and ruin everything. Pack all the food on the top so it rides high and centered on the horse, thus keeping it safe from the fuel.

Glass bottles should be avoided. If broken, both you and your horse could be picking slivers out for days!

Alex helps me stow the breakables and perishables in rawhide panniers, plywood boxes that have been covered with cow hide, hair side out to keep them from rubbing sores on the horse. These rigid-sided panniers offer more protection for fragile contents when an animal decides it can squeeze between two trees that aren't quite wide enough to accommodate horse and pack load.

Once we balance each set of panniers for equal weight, we hoist them on the sawbucks, cover them with a canvas manti (tarp) and secure the load by tying a basket hitch around everything.

By late morning, we hit the trail.

We carry lunches in our saddle bags, eating as we ride rather than stopping for a meal. Even those "cruel masters" Marcy mentioned journeyed without "nooning" as nineteenth century travelers called it. However, not for the same reason. "If the mules are suffered to halt," Marcy logged, "they are apt to lie down, and it is very difficult for them, with their loads, to rise; besides, they are likely to strain themselves in their efforts to do so." As for us, we simply believe it isn't fair to the animals to make them bear the pack weights while we humans take a break.

During the afternoon, we do make a couple of stops to adjust the order of the pack string. Sandy won't behave unless she leads. Blaze dislikes bringing up the rear. On the other hand, Smoke, an easy-going gray, doesn't seem to care where Teri puts him. Unfortunately, Boulderdash, the big Morgan she rides, takes exception when Sandy starts nipping his tail. Each time Teri disciplines the mule, Sandy lays her ears back, pouts, and slows up until it forces Teri to practically drag her along for a while. But none of the animals rodeo (the equivalent of equine kick-boxing), so we declare the day a success.

Later, we amble into a medium-sized meadow filled with wild flowers and tall grasses. A creek gurgles nearby, an inviting sound. Birds chatter in the cluster of pines that ring the field. A perfect place to set up camp.

As with goatpacking, the first order of business is to tend to the animals. Untying the basket hitches, we remove the loads—mantis, panniers, and sawbucks. Next, we give the animals a good brushing and lead them to the creek for a long drink.

Sir William Drummond Steward hired a young artist named Alfred Jacob Miller to make on-the-spot sketches of the scenery and events of his expedition to what people in 1837 called the "Far West," which included this area of the Wind River mountains. Along with his drawings and water colors, Miller kept a journal. In one entry, he noted asking permission to pay another member of the party to tend to his

Onyx on a picket at a horse camp in a high mountain meadow.
Photo credit: Jeff Corney.

horse in the evenings. Steward refused on the ground it would be a "breach of discipline and favoritism."

So Miller sketched a picture he labeled "Picketing Horses." The method has changed little since the notation that accompanied the drawing. Each man caught his horse "by the lariat (a rope trailing on the ground from his neck), and leads him to a good bed of grass, where a picket is driven, and here he is secured for the night, the lariat permitting him to graze to the extent of a circle twenty-five feet in diameter."

We use a rope with a leather belt on one end that is buckled around the horse's front hoof instead of attaching it to his halter because it's very easy for a horse to get a foot tangled in a halter and hurt itself. The thirty foot rope's other end is attached to a corkscrew-shaped rod we twist into the ground rather than pound in.

Thus we stake out Boulderdash and Prancer, the dominate horses in the group. We hobble the rest (two leather belts with a short section of chain between them that is buckled to both front pasterns). Sandy, being the leader of the pack string, also gets a bell around her neck. Last, we distribute some alfalfa pellets for them to munch on along with the meadow grass. Then we fix and eat our Mule Meatloaf, not made from the real thing like it was in the nineteenth century.

During what turned into a fifty-two day "starvation march" on a campaign against the Sioux and Northern Cheyenne in 1876, calvary soldiers under General George Crook's command stayed alive until a detachment returned with supplies by boiling and roasting their pack mules.

Day One Dinner Recipes:

Mule Meatloaf
1 lb. ground beef
1 onion, chopped
1 bell pepper, chopped
4 stalks celery, chopped
2 cloves garlic, crushed
1/3 c. catsup
3 T. water
20 saltine crackers, crushed
2 egg whites
1 t. pepper
1 t. basil
2 T. parsley flakes
1/2 t. hickory smoke salt

Combine all ingredients. Shape into patties. Freeze on a cookie sheet. When completely frozen, stack in a zipper plastic bag with pieces of waxed paper between patties. If you like catsup on top of your meatloaf, pack a zipper bag containing 2 c. additional catsup.

Rumpstrap
3 potatoes
1–16 oz. can sliced peaches in juice
    Wash and dry potatoes. Store in a net bag. Pack peaches.

Panniers Pecan Delight
1 c. caramels
1/2 c. raisins
3 c. crisp rice cereal
2 T. margarine
    Take the wrapper off each caramel and bag. Store raisins and cereal together. Bag margarine separately.

In the field preparation
    Fry patties in a covered skillet. Flip. Slice potatoes thin. Open peaches. Drain juice into the smaller pot. Add potatoes and about a cup of water. Cover and boil. Stir frequently, adding more water if necessary to cook potatoes. When tender, add peaches. Top meatloaf with catsup and serve with potatoes.
    Melt 1 T. margarine in the large pot over medium heat. Add caramels, stirring constantly until melted. Throw in raisins and cereal. Stir until coated. Coat skillet with 1 T. margarine. Spread mixture into it and allow it to set up for five minutes. Cut into bite-sized pieces. Eat while still warm. If any is leftover, heat slightly in the skillet before eating as the caramel will harden when cool.
    THIS MEAL needs no adaptation for float or goat trips. For backpacking, dehydrate meat, vegetables, and peaches. Substitute 3 tomatoes (chopped and dried) for catsup, omit eggs (replace with additional water) and instead of making patties, cook it up in a large pot with enough water to make it like stew.

After dinner, we move the picketed Boulderdash and Prancer, for as Miller wrote, "all [the grass] is eaten down pretty close by morning." Since Sandy has shown herself to be something of a trouble-maker, Teri stakes the mule out for the night as well. The others we tie to a highline, a rope tied between two trees that acts like a hitching post for the horses.

DAY TWO

BREAKFAST

Mexican Sombrero
Hot Chocolate

TRAIL LUNCH

Cold Cuts with Chinese Hot Mustard
Peanut butter and chopped prunes
Fresh fruit

DINNER

Campfire Beans
Broccoli and Corn
Watermelon

DAY TWO

Being the cook, whether hired or volunteer, offers a great advantage on backcountry trips. Everybody loves the cook, provided the food tastes good! Even Miller discovered this. Beside a picture entitled "Breakfast at Sunrise," he recorded, "The sketch represents 'our mess' at the morning meal—Jean who is pouring out coffee, seems to our hungry eyes more graceful than Hebe disposing Nectar, although he is more shapless than a log of wood."

We express similar feelings as we watch Alex dishing up our breakfast of Mexican Sombrero, except for the bit about the wood!

Day Two Breakfast Recipe:

Mexican Sombrero

6 eggs
1 onion, chopped
1–7 oz. can Salsa Verde (or a tomato-based salsa for less heat)
2 c. Swiss cheese, diced
8 whole wheat flour tortillas
1 T. margarine

Dice cheese and bag. Freeze tortillas, keeping frozen until ready to leave. (It keeps them fresher longer in the field.) Store eggs in a plastic container designed for carrying into the backcountry. It's better to pack onions in either a paper or mesh bag. Storing them for any length of time in plastic promotes rot. Bag margarine separately. Don't forget the salsa.

In the field preparation

Melt margarine in a skillet. Chop the onion and saute in margarine while beating the eggs in a large bowl. Add eggs, salsa, and cheese to onions. Cover and cook over medium heat. Flip once cheese melts and eggs begin to brown. Remove tortillas from package and warm on top of the skillet lid as the eggs cook. When eggs are done, cut into six wedges and place on top of the tortillas. Serve with hot chocolate.

THIS MEAL needs no adaptation for float or goat trips. Since powdered eggs aren't an adequate substitute for fresh eggs, choose a suitable breakfast from the other types of trips if you don't want the added weight of carrying in the eggs.

Horses can cover thirty to forty miles a day unless forced to pick their way through rough, rocky terrain or high mountain passes. On this test run, we content ourselves with meandering through the low country of the Bridger National Forest, traveling less than half that distance each day.

Onyx's smooth walking gate lulls me with perpetual motion. Settling in my saddle, I watch the forest slip by. Snowcapped mountains on the horizon come into view every now and then between breaks in the pines. An occasional hawk screeches or scolding magpies vie with the muffled *thud clump* of hoofbeats in the dirt. Even Sandy plods along with the peaceful attitude of the place.

Our wanderings bring us to the Big Sandy River. It cuts through the landscape of pines and open grasslands, churning with the run-off from late springs snows. As we let the animals wade in and drink their fill, I'm reminded of Miller's "Scene on 'Big Sandy' River." "The sketch may be said to represent a small slice of an Indian paradise—Indian women, horses, a stream of water, shade trees, and the broad prairie to the right," he declared. Glancing over my shoulder at riders, mounts, and pack animals, I see the tradition of what Miller drew and wrote about.

One by one the horses lift their heads, their thirst satiated, and continue across the river.

River crossing leading a pack mule. Photo credit: Wyoming Travel Commission.

About an hour down the trail, we meet up with a couple of hikers leading a pack horse that hauls all their gear like prospectors during the gold rush days. Similar to goatpacking, some outfitters rent horses to people who enjoy hiking, but prefer not to carry a backpack. This also cuts down on the number of horses needed on an animal-assisted trip, lessening the environmental impact.

The hikers stop, stepping off the trail so when we pass by, our horses won't spook at any unexpected sight or movement. Blaze whinnies and Dancer snorts at these newcomers. Onyx nearly twists his head off, peering back at them in a sizing-up manner.

The afternoon grows warm. With the heat comes the mosquitos and the biting flies. Before long, the animals start to fidget. Knowing the restlessness will soon turn into irritability, Teri guides the pack string off the trail and into a shaded patch of pines. She dismounts, ties the animals to the trees, then takes a plastic bottle with a trigger nozzle from her saddlebags as the rest of us follow suit.

Boulderdash lets Teri spray the pungent fly repellent on his coat without so much as a twitch of his skin. Sandy, on the other hand, acts like she's being doused with acid, shying away every time Teri comes near, stomping her hooves, trying to kick.

Joy pulls a faded bandana from her pocket. She drenches it with fly spray while Teri and Kirk take up positions on each side of Sandy's head. The two hold the mule steady, murmuring in soothing tones as Joy wipes the cloth over Sandy's neck and legs. Easy-going Smoke also takes exception to the stuff and must be coaxed into standing still by Alex and me while Teri rubs him down.

In the 1800s, travelers didn't worry about biting insects on themselves, their animals, or even in the food. Bread recipes mentioned in Oregon Trail journals occasionally described how dough would turn black from swarms of mosquitoes getting stuck in it. Since cooks couldn't prevent this, they simply baked the bread, mosquitoes and all.

That evening when we select a campsite in one of the mountains' abundant meadows, we look forward to a bug-free dinner.

Day Two Dinner Recipes:

Campfire Beans
2–15 1/2 oz. cans kidney beans
1 lb. summer sausage
1/4 c. powdered milk
1 t. nutmeg
1/4 c. sugar

Mix milk, nutmeg, and sugar and bag together. Store beans and sausage separately.

Broccoli and Corn

1–16 oz. pkg. frozen broccoli

1–16 oz. pkg frozen corn

Dehydrate the vegetables and pack in a zipper plastic bag.

Watermelon

1 watermelon

Put the whole melon in a plastic bag just before leaving on the trip. (If stored too long in plastic, it will promote rotting. But the plastic will protect other items in the pannier should the melon burst.)

In the field preparation

Rehydrate the broccoli and corn. Bring a pot of water to boil for cooking the vegetables and for hot drinks. Slice summer sausage and combine it with the other Campfire Beans ingredients in a skillet. When the broccoli and corn are reconstituted, add them to the boiling water and cook, covered, over medium heat until tender. Slice and serve the watermelon for dessert.

THIS MEAL needs no adaptation for goat and float trips. For backpacking, substitute dehydrated beans and bulk sausage that has been browned before drying. Replace the watermelon with another lightweight dessert.

DAY THREE

BREAKFAST

Whole Wheat Slam-Johns
Fresh Oranges

TRAIL LUNCH

Deviled ham and chopped dill pickles
Hot Carrot Spread
Fresh fruit

DINNER

Salmon Manti
Mushroom Stuff
Fruit Cache

DAY THREE

Women on the Oregon Trail sometime referred to pancakes as "slam-johns." The *American Frugal Housewife,* published in 1832, instructed cooks to add flour until "the spoon moves round with difficulty. If they are thin, they are apt to soak fat. Have the fat in your skillet boiling hot, and drop them in with a spoon. . . The more fat they are cooked in, the less they soak."

Teri expertly flips our slam-johns this cloudy morning, creating stacks which disappear as fast as they appear.

Day Three Breakfast Recipe:

Whole Wheat Slam-Johns
1 c. whole wheat flour
2 T. powdered buttermilk
1/2 t. baking powder
1 t. salt
2 T. sugar
1 1/4 c. water
2 T. margarine
Mix and bag all ingredients except margarine.

In the field preparation

While coffee water heats, mix 3/4 c. cold water with dry ingredients to make a batter. Melt some of the margarine in the skillet, enough to coat the bottom. Spoon batter into hot skillet. Cook, covered, over medium heat. Flip once after bottom browns and top gets firm, 2–4 minutes per side. If the outside is cooking too fast and inside is still raw, lower heat. Serve with honey or molasses and fresh oranges. Makes 12.

THIS MEAL needs no adaptation to be suitable for all types of trips.

Day Three Lunch Recipe:

Hot Carrot Spread
1/4 head cabbage
3 carrots
1/2 c. raisins
Hot English Mustard
    Store ingredients separately.

In the field preparation
Shred cabbage and carrots. Mix in raisins and enough mustard to hold mixture together. Spread on bread, tortillas, rolls, or bagels.
    THIS LUNCH is suitable for goat and float trips.

Clouds boil like oatmeal in a big gray pot. A few sprinkles announce the forthcoming rain, forcing us to break camp in a hurry before everything gets wet. Once we get the horses saddled and the panniers loaded, the canvas mantis protect the contents from the now persistent, cold drizzle.

I don my cowboy hat and slicker, just two pieces of the quintessential and very fashionable cowboy apparel. But cowboy hats, boots, and slickers all have their roots planted in the practical.

Good felt hats guard against the bright sunshine and shield your eyes from wind-blown sand or snow. The compressed felt also repels water, and the brim's wide shape acts like a gutter, keeping frigid rain water from dripping down your face and the back of your neck.

Pointed-toe construction of cowboy boots allow for quick access into the stirrup of a wheeling horse, while the heel stops your foot from slipping through the stirrup and becoming caught.

Then there's the slicker. Especially designed for horseback use, the mustard-colored 1880s Pommel Slicker, also called a "Fishskin" or "Tower" saddle coat, was made of a heavy canvas or duck material that had been waterproofed with linseed oil. Other than utilizing modern rain-repellent fabric, today's slicker differs little from the original pattern. The long split up the back allows the ankle-length coat to cover the entire saddle, as well as the rider. So I maintain a dry seat even when it starts to pour in earnest.

Before long, we begin to look like extras in a Clint Eastwood western. Rain streams from our hats each time we glance down. The horses hang their heads. Their coats darken and slick down with moisture. It beads on the canvas mantis and rolls off the sides in mini-waterfalls. But our food remains dry.

Horse hooves *ssquish* in the mud as the deluge splatters against the ground. Each time one of the packs rubs against tree boughs, it releases the aromatic pine scent into the damp air.

When the wind changes, blowing freezing rain down from the north, we stop and make camp in the first patch of grassland we come to.

Alonzo Delano, one of countless thousands of forty-niners struck with gold fever, faced a similar situation on his way to California, which he wrote about in *Life on the Plains and at the Diggings* (1854). After a stormy day where "it seemed as if a water spout was discharging its floods upon us," Delano went on to note, "our stoves were put into our tents, and the covers of boxes, or stray pieces of wood in the wagons, were used to start a fire, and then buffalo chips were heaped upon the stoves until they got dry enough to burn, and in this way we contrived to do our cooking."

Delano finished the day's entry with "distance, nothing" which sums up our day as well.

Teri sets up the two-burner stove in the vestibule of our tent. I turn the camp table on its side and place it so that it acts as a windshield against the blowing rain. Nevertheless, drops still fly in and land on the heating skillets of food and dance on the lids.

After we tend to the animals, everybody crowds into the tent, trying not to drip mud onto our meal as we squirm out of slickers and boots in the shelter of the vestibule and crawl inside. This kind of weather makes us wish for a wall tent which is about the size of a room in a small house.

Instead we pass pans, ingredients, utensils, bowls, silverware, and finally food back and forth like an assembly line at an auto plant. But it makes the meal just that much more enjoyable because everybody participates in the preparation of our salmon feast.

Salmon was either dried, smoked, pickled, or packed in salt to preserve it until after the Civil War, when canned foods became more readily available. Immigrant workers cleaned, boned, and packed salmon in cans by hand until 1882 when a machine took over this labor intensive job.

Day Three Dinner Recipes:

Salmon Manti
2–14 3/4 oz. cans salmon
2–10 3/4 oz. cans cream of asparagus soup
1 onion
4 T. Worcestershire sauce
2 t. dry mustard
1 t. garlic powder
3 c. spinach noodles
1 T. margarine
Combine Worcestershire sauce, dry mustard, and garlic powder in a plastic bottle. Store onion in a net bag. Bag noodles and margarine separately. Pack cans of salmon and soup.

Mushroom Stuff

12 big mushrooms
1/2 bell pepper, chopped fine
1 1/2 slices bread
3 T. Parmesan cheese
1/4 c. margarine

Remove stems from mushrooms. Chop the stems. Dehydrate mushroom caps and stems, bell pepper, and bread. When dry, crumble bread and bag with pepper, stems, and cheese. Store mushroom caps and margarine in two separate bags.

Fruit Cache

2–16 oz. can fruit cocktail in juice
1–11 oz. can Mandarin Orange segments
1/3 c. raisins

Bag raisins. Pack cans of fruit

In the field preparation

Rehydrate mushroom caps and the bell pepper mixture. Open salmon. Pour fish and juice into an empty plastic bag. Add Worcestershire sauce mixture. Seal and gently squeeze until mixed. Set aside. Bring a large pot of water to boil. Add noodles. Cook uncovered until done, about 12 minutes. Stir occasionally.

Meanwhile melt 1/4 c. margarine in the skillet. Pour in pepper mixture and blend. Spoon mixture into caps. Arrange in the skillet and cook over low heat for 15 minutes.

Chop onion. In smaller pot, melt 1 T. margarine and add onion. Stir over medium heat until tender. Add salmon mixture and soup. Cook until completely heated. Serve over drained noodles.

Open cans of fruit. Add raisins. Serve.

THIS MEAL needs no adaptation for float or goat trips. The Mushroom Stuff also needs no adaptation for backpacking. The Salmon Manti and Fruit Cache, however is not suitable for backpacking unless you don't mind the extra weight of canned foods. Dried fruit mix can be substituted for Fruit Cache.

DAY FOUR

BREAKFAST

Depuyer Biscuits
Timberline Gravy
Coffee

TRAIL LUNCH

Sardine Sling
Parmesan Half Hitch
Fresh fruit

DINNER

Horsepacker's Pie
A & P Barrel

DAY FOUR

"A cold wind blew this morning," wrote Delano the morning after the rain storm. "The sky was overcast with clouds, and the gloom and air of November, rather than the genial warmth of spring, hung over us."

We wake to snow, which poses a completely different cooking problem for Kirk. All twigs are either buried in the snow or soaked from yesterday's rain. Rather than wasting fuel drying twigs in a pan on the stove, Kirk elects to make flip biscuits. Instead of forming half inch rounds of dough (as called for in the recipe), he flattens each biscuit until it resembles a silver dollar-sized pancake and places them in the skillet over a low heat. Halfway through the "baking" time, he turns them to cook both sides. Thus we have an adequate alternative to baked biscuits for our breakfast.

Plains Indians, whose primary food source came from the buffalo, found their own substitute for biscuits, called "depuyer" by the mountain men. Indians took the ridge of fatty tissue that ran along the buffalo's backbone, dipped it in hot grease for half a minute, then hung it up inside the lodge to dry and smoke for twelve hours. Pieces of depuyer were cut from the main strap and served with fresh or dried meat.

Day Four Breakfast Recipes:

Depuyer Biscuits
2 1/3 c. flour
1 t. salt
1 t. baking powder
1 t. baking soda
4 T. powdered buttermilk
3 1/2 T. margarine
    Bag together all ingredients except margarine.

Timberline Gravy

1/2 lb. sausage

1/4 c. powdered milk

1 t. salt

2 1/2 T. flour

1 t. pepper

2 T. margarine

Brown sausage and dehydrate. Mix and bag powdered milk, salt, flour, and pepper. Bag sausage separately from margarine.

In the field preparation

Cut 3 1/2 T. margarine into biscuit mix. Add 3/4 c. cold water and squeeze to form soft dough. Pat into biscuits about 1/2 inch thick. Bake over low heat and lid fire for 10–12 minutes. Makes 14.

When biscuits are done, keep warm in insulated bowls. Melt 2 T. margarine in skillet. Add sausage and powdered milk mixture. Stir constantly while adding 2 c. of cold water. Bring to a boil, continuing to stir until gravy thickens. Serve over biscuits.

THIS MEAL needs no adaptation for any type of trip.

Day Four Lunch Recipes:

Sardine Sling

2–3.75 oz. cans sardines in mustard

1 T. horseradish

1 T. reconstituted lemon juice

1 t. paprika

Mix horseradish, lemon juice, and paprika together and bag. Pack cans of sardines.

Parmesan Half Hitch
1 c. Parmesan cheese
1/2 t. cayenne
1 T. Worcestershire sauce
2 T. margarine
    Mix cheese and cayenne and bag together. Store remaining ingredients separately.

In the field preparation
    For Sardine Sling, mash all ingredients together in plastic bags. Spread on bread, bagels, or rolls. For Parmesan Hitch, melt margarine; pour it and remaining ingredients in a plastic bag and mix by squeezing. Spread on bread, bagels, or rolls.
    THIS LUNCH is suitable for goat and float trips.

Horses stand with their backs to the storm, eyeing us warily as we break down camp. They paw through the accumulation to reach the meadow grass underneath. If we hadn't had to make do with a marginal pasture, we'd be tempted to just sit around the stove, drinking tea and telling stories, and wait out the storm. But the horses need better grazing.
    Large flakes fall fast and wet, obstructing sight and sound. Wind whips through the trees, shaking clumps from the limbs in the same manner the animals employ to rid themselves of the blankets of white lining their backs.
    Hampered by the snowfall, it takes us longer than normal to round up the herd. Onyx stamps his feet at my approach, but he doesn't bound away like Blaze and Smoke do at Teri's advance. Hobbles only slow horses down. These quick-witted equines swiftly learn how to hop across a field with the agility of jackrabbits. But once captured, they settle down into the dependable animals we rely on in the wilderness.

The journals of enlisted men and officers alike who saw field service in the West tell of the hardships faced by the soldiers and their animals during the Indian campaigns of the post-Civil War years. Ill-equiped for the elements, these frontier regulars counted on their horses and mules for survival. When a snowstorm blew in, the men pulled their horses' feed bags over their heads to protect their faces from the severe weather. Thus unable to see, the soldiers relied on the animals to find a way through the drifts to shelter.

We, too, seek shelter as the snow thickens, cocooning us in white. Reining the horses off the trail, we bushwhack through the trees for a shorter path to a decent meadow where the animals can paw their way through the snow to graze. Here we set up camp.

Once we get the animals taken care of for the night, everybody helps Joy hunt for dead twigs laying at the bases of the trees. The snow prevents us from finding enough to bake our Horsepacker's Pie. So she boils the sliced potatoes, adding the rehydrated meat and peas and cooks it until tender. Next she adds the canned mushroom soup. Meanwhile, she heats the tortillas in the skillet over low. Leaving one in the bottom, Joy pours the meat and vegetable mixture over it, then tops the concoction with the other tortilla—not unlike what the pioneers did.

When a scarcity of burnable fuel forced frontier cooks to improvise, meat and vegetable pies were boiled with either dumplings or bread crumbs as the crust, which they called the "paste."

Day Four Dinner Recipes:

Horsepacker's Pie
2 potatoes
1 lb. ground beef

1–16 oz. pkg. frozen peas
1–10 1/2 oz. can cream of mushroom soup
2 large tortillas
1 T. parsley flakes
2 t. onion powder
1 t. garlic powder
1 t. pepper
2 T. soy sauce
2 T. Worcestershire sauce
1 T. margarine

Brown ground beef. Dehydrate meat and peas. Wash and pat dry potatoes before packing them in a net bag. Mix and bag together the parsley, onion powder, garlic powder, and pepper. Store soy sauce and Worcestershire sauce in plastic bottles. Pack margarine separately.

A & P Barrel
1–16 oz. can apricots in juice
1–20 oz. can pineapple chunks in juice
20 graham crackers

Pack each item separately.

In the field preparation

While water boils for hot drinks, rehydrate the meat and peas. Slice potatoes very thin. Melt margarine in the skillet. Place one tortilla in the bottom. Lay the potato slices on the tortilla. Add peas, then ground meat. Sprinkle pepper mixture, soy, and Worcestershire sauce over meat and smear soup over the top. Lay other tortilla on top. Cover. Bake over low heat and a lid fire for 30–35 minutes.

Open apricots and pineapple. Mix together in a pot. Crush crackers over the top and serve.

THIS MEALS needs no adaptation for goat or float trips. For backpacking, substitute dehydrated potatoes and leave out the soy sauce and Worcestershire sauce (unless you don't mind carrying the extra weight) and serve dried fruits for dessert.

DAY FIVE

BREAKFAST

Double Diamond Mincemeat
Coffee

TRAIL LUNCH

Deviled ham and chopped dill pickles
Crab Pardner
Fresh fruit

DINNER

Mountain Meadow Eggplant
Shifty Eyed
End of the Rope
Tea

DAY FIVE

In the sixteenth century, cooks preserved meat by making mincemeat. They chopped the meat (frequently tongue) very fine; added large quantities of spices such as mace, cloves, and nutmeg; sugar; chopped suet (fat); fruits such as raisins, currants, apples, lemons, and oranges; rosewater; and liquor (usually brandy or wine). This mixture was packed into crocks and salt sprinkled over the top. After covering the stone jars, cooks stored them in the root cellar.

Day Five Breakfast Recipe:

Double Diamond Mincemeat
4 slices dried beef
1 c. mixed dried fruit
1/4 c. nuts, chopped
1 c. flour
1/4 c. brown sugar
1 t. baking powder
1 t. salt
2 T. powdered milk
4 T. margarine

Purchase thin sliced dried beef in a jar. Bag with fruit and nuts. Mix flour, sugar, baking powder, salt, and powdered milk and bag together. Store margarine separately.

In the field preparation

Bring beef mixture to a boil in 1/3 c. water in a covered pot. Boil for 2 minutes. Melt margarine in the skillet. Mix dry ingredients with 1 c. cold water to form a thick batter. Pour over melted margarine. Add fruit. Bake over low heat and a lid fire for 30 minutes, rotating for even cooking.

THIS MEAL needs no adaptation for any of the types of trips.

Day Five Lunch Recipe:

Crab Pardner
1–6 oz. can crab meat
1 T. lemon juice
1 T. margarine
1/4 t. paprika
    Pack each item separately.

In the field preparation
    Mash all ingredient together in a plastic bag. Serve on bread, rolls, or tortillas.
    THIS LUNCH is suitable for goat and float trips.

From looking at this morning's sky, you'd never guess we'd had two full days of bad weather. Sunny, clear blue as far as the eye can see, and warm. Except under the dense forest, the snow melts away like a ghostly reminder.

Although sloppy, it proves an easy walk-out day for the horses. This morning Teri decides to break up the pack string, and we swop off leading Sandy, Blaze, and Smoke separately. The trio behaves well on individual lead ropes, following behind our mounts. Better than when strung together.

A few hours along the trail, we come upon a group of backpackers with a couple of dogs. Knowing that our horses might frighten easily, the hikers move off the downhill side of the trail and tell their dogs to be quiet while we pass.

As I draw near, one of the dogs starts to whine and shake. Onyx dances into a side step. I murmur reassuringly in his ear while the dog's owner restrains it. When Sandy, who is right behind me, reaches the dog, she snorts and kicks up her heels, but doesn't cause a scene or a rodeo. Thank goodness!

By late afternoon, we arrive at the roadhead and our waiting trailers. The horses and Sandy receive a big bucket of grain while we unload the panniers and stow the tack for the trip home.

The animals seem reluctant to enter the trailers in preparation for leaving. For that matter, so do we for as Reverend Stephen Riggs wrote in 1880, after he and his wife spent forty years in the West with the Sioux, "It has been marvelous in our eyes."

Day Five Dinner Recipes:

Mountain Meadow Eggplant
2 eggplants, sliced thin
Marinate for eggplant
2/3 c. mayonnaise
4 T. vinegar
2 T. lemon juice
2 t. salt
2 t. pepper
2 t. Worcestershire sauce
1 t. Tabasco

Blend together marinate. Soak eggplant in marinate for 24 hours. Pat dry before drying.

Shifty Eyed
1 pkg. frozen peas and carrots
1 pkg. white sauce mix

Dehydrate peas and carrots. Do not thaw first. Bag separately from the sauce mix.

End of the Rope
1/2 lb. cheese
1 T. margarine
pretzels

In the field preparation

Reconstitute eggplant, peas, and carrots. After making hot drinks, pour 1/2 c. boiling water in saucepan and add peas and carrots. Cover. Bring to boil over high heat. Remove from stove. Place eggplant and 1 c. of cold water in the skillet. Cook over medium heat until tender, adding more water as needed. Double decker peas and carrots on top of eggplant (unless you have a two-burner stove).

When ready for dessert, slice cheese thin and melt in margarine in a pot over low heat. Dip in pretzels.

THIS MEAL need no adaptation for any of the types of trips.

DAY SIX

BREAKFAST

Molasses Mix
Coffee

TRAIL LUNCH

Hard Salami with sliced Cheddar and horseradish
Peanut butter with banana chips
Fresh fruit

DINNER

Rope Jerker
Camp Custard
Tea

DAY SIX

Day Six Breakfast Recipe:

Molasses Mix
1 c. flour
1/2 c. buckwheat flour
1 t. baking powder
1 t. baking soda
1 t. salt
3 T. powdered buttermilk
1/2 t. allspice
1 c. brown sugar, firmly packed
1/2 c. raisins
1 egg
1/2 c. molasses
1/4 c. margarine
       Mix and bag together first nine ingredients. Store egg in carton. Bag margarine separately. Put molasses in plastic bottle.

In the field preparation
       After coffee water heats, melt margarine in skillet. Pour it, molasses, and 1/2 c. water into bag of flour mixture. Add egg. Reseal and squeeze gently to mix. Pour the thick batter into skillet. Cover and bake over low with a lid fire for 45–60 minutes.
       THIS MEAL needs no adaptation for float or goat trips. For backpacking, replace egg with extra water. (Cake will be heavier and less moist.)

Day Six Dinner Recipes:

Rope Jerker
1 lb. sausage
2 apples, sliced thin
1 onion, chopped
4 stalks celery, chopped
1/2 t. cinnamon
1/4 t. cayenne
1 t. caraway seed
2 c. spinach noodles
1 T. cornstarch

Brown sausage. Dehydrate meat, apples, onion, and celery. Bag these with cinnamon, cayenne, and caraway seed. Bag cornstarch and noodles in two separate bags.

Camp Custard
1–2.9 oz. box custard mix
1/4 c. powdered milk
1 egg

Bag custard mix and powdered milk together. Store egg in carton.

In the field preparation

Rehydrate sausage, apples, onion, and celery. Make hot drinks. Add 1 c. water to sausage mixture and bring to boil over medium heat in a covered pot. Cook until tender.

Meanwhile, collect small bowls. Blend custard mixture, egg, and 2 c. water. Heat over medium until it boils. Remove from heat. Pour into bowls and set aside.

When sausage mixture is tender. Bring liquid level up to two cups again and return to a boil. Add noodles. Cook over medium heat until done, about 15 minutes.

In 1/3 c. water add cornstarch, mix well. Stir into sausage mixture. Boil 1 minute. Serve.

THIS MEAL needs no adaptation for float and goat trip. For backpacking, make custard without egg.

DAY SEVEN

BREAKFAST

Bellmeal
Coffee

TRAIL LUNCH

Corned beef hash and horseradish
Dates chopped with almonds
Fresh fruit

DINNER

Sawbucks
Horseshoes

DAY SEVEN

Day Seven Breakfast Recipe:

Bellmeal
1/2 c. oats
1 t. salt
1/4 cantaloupe
    Dehydrate cantaloupe. Bag separately from oats and salt.

In the field preparation
    Bring 1 1/4 c. cold water and cantaloupe chips to boil in a covered pot over high heat. Add oatmeal and cook 2 minutes. THIS MEAL need no adaptation for any type of trip.

Day Seven Dinner Recipes:

Sawbucks
1–10 oz. pkg. frozen corn
5 chicken franks, sliced thin
6 tomatoes, chopped
1 onion, chopped
1 bell pepper, chopped
4 c. egg noddles
1/4 t. cayenne pepper
1 t. chili powder
    Dehydrate corn, franks, tomatoes, onion, and bell pepper. Do not thaw corn first. When dry, bag with pepper and chili powder. Store noodles separately.

Horseshoes
12 T. chunky peanut butter
1 T. cocoa
3 T. sugar

Mix cocoa and sugar and bag. Purchase a small plastic jar of peanut butter for the field.

In the field preparation

Rehydrate meat and vegetables. In a large, covered pot, bring meat and vegetables to boil in an additional 2 c. of cold water. When food is tender, add more water to bring level up to 2 1/2 c. When it is boiling again, add noodles. Cook over medium heat until done, about 15 minutes.

Drop peanut butter by teaspoons into cocoa sugar mix one at a time. Roll around until the outside is coated. Pop them into your mouth. (Kids love to make these!)

THIS MEAL needs no adaptation for any type of trip.

The Butte of the Cross.
Photo credit: Sierra Adare.

SEVEN DAYS OF FLOAT TRIP MEALS

Of all outdoor journeys, float trips offer a unique advantage. The water carries all the weight. So if your taste buds veer toward champagne and caviar and you can squeeze them in the ice chest, go for it! You only have to worry about lugging that chest into and out of the boat. Float trips accord the widest range of eating possibilities as ice chests keep perishable foods fresh and drinks cold for several days. There's nothing like kicking off your sneakers, letting your feet dangle in the cool water, leaning back against a soft pile of sleeping bags, munching on crisp cucumber and watercress sandwiches and listening to ice cubes *clink* in your tea while the world quietly drifts by.

River trips run for the course of an afternoon up to a week or more. Therefore, seven days' worth of meals follow.

Float lunches

With the exertion level more or less comparable to goat-packing, plan on about 1/3 pound of lunchables per person per day. Choose from the list below or from any of the other trail lunches listed in this cookbook. Include a supply of fresh fruit, fruit juices, and sodas, as well. Serve the following fillers on breads, assorted crackers, muffins, tortillas, bagels, or rolls.

Sandwich and cracker fillers

Apricots (canned) mashed with chopped walnuts

Baked beans mashed with catsup

Carrots (raw) grated with mashed canned peas

Cream cheese with sliced cucumbers and water-cress

Hard boiled eggs with stewed tomatoes

Peanut butter and chopped sweet pickles

Peanut butter with chopped dates

Pineapple (canned, crushed) with chopped pecans

Raisins chopped with orange sections

Salmon (canned) with tomato slices and Dijon mustard

Lady of the Lake Lunch (see recipe below)

Smoked sausages mashed with 1–7 oz. can Salsa Verde

Turkey Day Spread (recipe below)

Trin-Alcove Sandwich Filler (recipe below)

Hints for taking fresh foods into the field

Store onions and potatoes in net bags (like onions come in at the store). Do not seal them in plastic bags as it will promote sprouting.

Store apples and oranges separately as they each give off gases that aid in spoiling the other variety of fruit.

Cover ice chests with tarps, duffel bags, or sleeping bags to keep them out of the direct sunlight.

Since frequent opening of an ice chest causes the ice to melt quicker, put all perishable food and drink items for the first day in one ice chest. Store the second day's perishable food and drinks in a second chest, etc., and don't open until necessary.

Tape shut all but the first day's ice chest with duct tape and number each chest in order of use. This keeps the chests from accidently coming open if turned over, plus stops people from digging into the wrong food chest by mistake.

Use blocks of ice rather than cubes for all but the first two days since block ice takes longer to melt.

To keep bread products from turning soggy, store them in plastic containers with airtight lids on top of the ice.

To avoid the possibility of losing all your food should a boat flip over, divide ice chests up between all the boats.

Supply list (7 days)

Baking Staples:
1–10 oz. box baking powder
1–16 oz. box baking soda
1 lb. blue cornmeal
1–5 lb. sack flour
1–lb. can powdered buttermilk
1–25.6 oz. box powdered milk
1–6 oz. bag semi-sweet chocolate chips
1–5 lb. sack sugar

Canned Goods:
2–2 oz. cans anchovies
1–10 oz. can baby clams in water
1–5 oz. can bamboo shoots
1–2.25 oz. chopped black olives
1–4 oz. can chopped green chiles
1–27 oz. can whole green chiles
1–16 oz. can jellied cranberry sauce
1–16 oz. can peach halves in juice
1–16 oz. can sliced peaches in juice
1–20 oz. can pineapple chunks in juice
1–20 oz. can pineapple rings in juice
1–16 oz. can tomato sauce
2–29 oz. cans tomato sauce
1–5 oz. can water chestnuts

Breads/Crackers/Cereals:
1 pkg. assorted individual boxes of cereal
1 box crisp rice cereal
4 bagels
4 English muffins
1 loaf sourdough bread
1 lb. box graham crackers

Dried Fruit/Vegetables/Nuts:
1–2 oz. pkg. almond slivers
1 lb. chopped walnuts
1 container candied fruits
1–8 oz. box chopped dates
1–14 oz. bag coconut flakes
1–1 lb. box raisins

Fresh Fruit:
3 apples
2 bananas
2 lbs. grapes
1 honeydew melon
6 oranges
4 tomatoes

Fresh Vegetables:
2 bell peppers
1 lb. carrots
1 bunch celery
1 cucumber
1 clove garlic
1 eggplant
2 green chiles
1 bunch green onions
1 lb. mushrooms
1 lb. okra
6 onions
12 potatoes
2 yellow squash

Frozen Food:
1–16 oz. pkg. San Francisco style vegetables

Meat/Milk/Margarine/Cheese/Eggs:
1/2 lb. bacon
1 lb. beef
1 lb. ham (1/2 lb. sliced paper thin)
1–6 oz. pkg. thin sliced turkey lunch meat
1 1/2 lbs. turkey sausage
4 whole chicken breasts
1–8 oz. pkg. cream cheese

1 lb. Monterey Jack cheese
1/2 lb. Myzithra cheese
1 1/2 dozen eggs
2–12 oz. cans evaporated milk
1 1/2 lbs. margarine
1 qt. olive oil

Rice/Noodles:
1 lb. brown rice
1–12 oz. pkg. egg noodles
1–7 oz. pkg. rice sticks
1–22 oz. pkg. spaghetti

Sauce & Other Mixes/Drinks/Speciality Items:
1 bottle soy sauce
1 bottle Worcestershire sauce
1–8 oz. can Amaretto flavored coffee drink
1–1.58 oz. anchovy paste
1 jar beef bouillon cube
1 can beer
1–3 1/2 oz. jar caviar
1 jar Chinese Hot Mustard
1 qt. cranberry juice
2–6 oz. custard style strawberry yogurt
1 lb. jar honey
1–16 oz. jar maraschino cherries
1–1 lb. bag miniature marshmallows
1 bottle molasses
1–10 oz. jar peach jam
1 bottle ranch dressing
60 assorted tea bags, coffee, soda pop (optional),
　　　fruit juice (optional)

Spices:
1 container allspice
1 container cayenne pepper
1 container cinnamon
1 container cumin
1 container dry mustard
1 container coarse black pepper
1 container garlic powder
1 container ginger
1 container ground cloves
1 container mace
1 container onion powder
1 container parsley flakes
1 container pepper
1 container salt
1 container thyme

DAY ONE

BREAKFAST

Ham Haystack
Myzithra Cheese
Sourdough Bread
Coffee

LUNCH

Carrots (raw) grated with mashed canned peas
Cream cheese with sliced cucumbers and watercress
Fresh Fruit
Juice or soda

DINNER

River Runner's Chicken
San Rafael Cake
Tea

DAY ONE

*July 13—This afternoon our way is through
a valley with cottonwood groves on either
side. The river is deep, broad, and quiet.*
          —John Wesley Powell

John Wesley Powell, a geologist, led the first expedition down the Green and Colorado Rivers in 1869. On July 13, the four boats in the expedition pulled ashore for an afternoon break about five miles south of where we will put in at the Green River State Park in Utah.

Powell kept a daily journal on long, narrow strips of brown paper which he bound in sole leather. When he published his log in 1895, he maintained he hadn't undertaken the exploration for adventure, but "purely for scientific purposes." But we, on the other hand, set out on a rainy May day to retrace 120 miles of his trip from Green River, Utah to just past the confluence of the Green and the Colorado solely for adventure.

The 1869 crew consisted of ten men, not a greenhorn among them. Experience in our group of eight ranges from long-time white water runners to weekend floaters to a never-been-in-a-boat beginner. Alan and Bobby, cousins, want to test the waters as a team before they tackle the white water through the Grand Canyon. Ty and Erin figure a canoe trip down what river runners call the "Serene Green" will make a memorable honeymoon. Lance, a businessman, loves the idea of a week in the inaccessible Canyonlands. Then there's Ron, our guide who grew up on the river. And me, the hired cook.

The gang shuttles vehicles and boat trailers over to Moab, fifty-two miles from Green River and arranges for a jet boat to meet us at the confluence. Seven days from now, it will haul us and the canoes sixty miles up the Colorado to our waiting cars.

I stay behind to finish packing the food, adding a last bit of ice, taping down the chests, and marking the ration days.

Early in the 1869 trip, Powell took the rations for granted, not even listing the amount of food taken on board. Instead he wrote, "we take with us rations deemed sufficient to last ten months." Only later, when they ran into hardships did meals become the subject of journal entries.

By the time our crew returns, I have breakfast ready.

Day One Breakfast Recipe:

Ham Haystack
1/2 lb. paper-thin sliced ham
4 T. course black pepper
1 T. allspice
sourdough bread

Mix pepper and allspice. Sprinkle some over each slice of ham, gently patting into the meat. Stack slices. Freeze. Also freeze 1 loaf of sourdough bread. Pack cheese.

In the field preparation

While waters boils for coffee, layer some ham on bread slices. Serve with cheese.

THIS MEAL requires no adaptation for use on horse or goat trips as a first day breakfast. It's suitable for a first day breakfast on a backpack trip if you don't mind some extra weight.

Although we pack all gear in plastic garbage bags, we still bundle everything in "dry bags" obtained from the army surplus store before stowing them under tarps in the canoes. Cameras and film go in watertight ammo boxes. Then we tie everything to the boats just in case one of the four canoes flips over. Ropes offer peace of mind. So does dividing the food among the four boats just as Powell did.

Eating a hurried lunch, we finally get underway.

Slickers protect our bodies from a persistent rain. We continually "swab the deck" with thick sponges, but our sneakers soak up the cold water like thirsty desert travelers. The dreary sky washes out the landscape, all but eradicating the distant cliffs on the horizon. Raindrops dimple the river. Wind kicks miniature waves against the boat hulls.

Since none of us have canoed together before, each team concentrates on gaining a rhythm to paddling in sync. The boats fishtail in a few near misses until we get it figured out.

Thunder ricochets off the sandstone butte, sounding ominous. Then the lightning starts. It discharges over Dellenbaugh Butte, named after Frederick Dellenbaugh, one of the young men who accompanied Powell on his second expedition in 1871.

By general consensus, we decide to call it a day and pull in near where the San Rafael River streams into the Green. Alan and Bobby help Ron off-load gear, while Ty, Erin, and Lance put up tents on wet sand.

I set up the two-burner stove under my folding table instead of on it and begin heating water for hot drinks. At least we'll eat, unlike Powell's crew who had to "weather out" a night of storms with no dinner. The next morning, Powell wrote that they had to "search for some time to find a few sticks of driftwood, just sufficient to boil a cup of coffee."

All the driftwood littering the beach is soaked. So when it comes time to bake our cake, I dump a layer of charcoal bricks over the top of the dutch oven and hold a lighter to them until they catch fire.

Day One Dinner Recipes:

River Runner's Chicken
4 whole chicken breasts, deboned and sliced
1–10 oz. jar peach jam
1/3 c. cranberry juice
1 T. soy sauce
1 t. ginger
1 T. Worcestershire sauce
1 t. pepper
1 t. dry mustard
1 t. garlic powder
1–16 oz. pkg. frozen San Francisco style vegetables
1–16 oz. can sliced peaches in juice
1 c. spaghetti
1 T. margarine
  Marinate chicken in next 8 ingredients for 24 hours. Freeze (don't drain marinate before freezing). Cook spaghetti in 2 qts. of boiling water, uncovered, for 12 minutes. Remove from heat. Drain. Mix cooked spaghetti with frozen vegetables and peaches in their juice, bag and freeze. Store margarine separately.

San Rafael Cake
1 1/3 c. flour
1/3 c. sugar
1 t. salt
1 t. baking powder
1 t. baking soda
1 T. ginger
1/2 c. chopped walnuts
1/4 c. powdered milk
1/4 c. plus 2 T. margarine
  Bag together all ingredients except margarine.

In the field preparation

Cut 1/4 c. margarine into dry cake ingredients. Add 1/3 c. cold water. Reseal bag and squeeze to mix. Makes a stiff dough. Melt 2 T. margarine in dutch oven or skillet. Spread dough in it. Cover. Bake over low heat with a lid fire for 25–30 minutes.

Melt margarine in the skillet. Add chicken, cover and cook until done. Stir in vegetable/fruit mixture, cooking over medium heat until vegetables are thoroughly heated. Serve.

AS AN OPTION on backpacking trips, grind, brown, and dehydrate the meat after marinating it. Also dry the vegetables. On horse or goat trips, this meal can be carried as is and served the first day out, or follow the backpacking option.

DAY TWO

BREAKFAST

Rushing River Bagels
Tea

LUNCH

Turkey Day Spread
Trin-Alcove Sandwich Filler
Fruit
Juice or soda

DINNER

Green Chile Relleno
Blue Corn Bread
Grapes

DAY TWO

July 15—Three side canyons enter at the same point. These canyons are very tortuous, almost closed in from view, and, seen from the opposite side of the river, they appear like three alcoves. We name this Trin-Alcove Bend... The right cove is a narrow, winding gorge, with overhanging walls, almost shutting out the light. The left is an amphitheater, turning spirally up, with overhanging shelves. A series of basins filled with water are seen at different altitudes as we pass by; huge rocks are piled below on the right, and overhead there is an arched ceiling.

—John Wesley Powell

In 1869, Powell's crew lived on coffee, sugar, jerky, and bacon that was too greasy to store in the rubber bags they used to supposedly keep the supplies dry. Despite precautions, the dried beans turned soggy from repeated dunkings in the muddy water, finally sprouting. Likewise, the apples began to ferment and flour for biscuits became hopelessly moldy. No wonder three of Powell's men mutinied!

Day Two Breakfast Recipe:

Rushing River Bagels
4 plain bagels
1–8 oz. pkg. cream cheese
1–3 1/2 oz. jar caviar
2 eggs
Pack each item separately.

In the field preparation

Bring eggs to a boil in a covered, large pot of cold water. Remove from heat and let stand for 20 minutes. Reserve water for tea. Lightly toast bagel halves face down in the skillet over medium heat. Spread 1/8 of the pkg. of cream cheese on each bagel half. Top with 1/8 of the caviar. Peel eggs. Slice. Place one slice of egg on top of each bagel half. Serve with tea.

THIS MEAL is only suitable as a first breakfast on either horse or goat trips. Substitute a less perishable breakfast for backpacking.

Pools high in the rocks of the Trin-Alcove have continued to provide river runners with a great source for fresh water since Powell first wrote about them. We fill every empty container, knowing we can't count on drinking from the Green. The river carries an estimated nineteen tons of silt per year, making the water the color and consistency of Cajun Gumbo. All those particles defeat filters, clogging them quickly. Even in 1869, Powell searched for pools of rain water standing in holes in the rocks to fill the team's need for drinking water.

Scrub brush shores and a series of variegated-colored buttes start to swell into canyon walls by afternoon—tall, formidable slabs of burnt orange sandstone. Neither Powell nor Dellenbaugh mentioned feeling dwarfed by the steep canyons, but I do. The others must feel it too, because chatter ceases. Only the song of a wren and the cry of a hawk intrude into the brooding quiet.

Due to the Green's placid flow, we spend much of the day dipping and swinging paddles. But as lunch time rolls around, we follow in a tradition begun by Powell's expedition. Steering the canoes toward each other until all crafts cluster side by side, we "tie" (Powell used real ropes for this) the boats together by draping our feet and arms into neighboring canoes to stop us from drifting apart. In this manner, we enjoy our lunch. (I had made sure the ingredients were easily accessible before we shoved off this morning.)

Day Two Lunch Recipes:

Turkey Day Spread
1–6 oz. pkg. thin sliced turkey lunch meat, shredded
1–16 oz. can jellied cranberry sauce
2 stalks celery, chopped fine
1 t. onion powder
  Blend well. Store in a zipper bag.

Trin-Alcove Sandwich Filler
2 apples, chopped fine
2 stalks celery, chopped fine
1/3 c. nuts, chopped
1–2.25 oz. can chopped black olives, drained
3 T. ranch dressing
  Mix all ingredients. Add more dressing if needed to hold spread together. Serve on bread or rolls.

THIS LUNCH is only suitable for a first day lunch on horse and goat trips, or for backpacking if you don't mind the extra weight.

In the late afternoon, twentieth century petroglyphs catch our attention and imagination—especially the ghostly image of the "The Face of the River." Its age and the identity of the artist who chiseled the face and flowing body high on a sandstone wall remains a mystery. The carving's bug-eyes watch the river far below, observing all who drift by on the slow current. He tallies their names in his River Register—the names and years of Green River expeditions etched in stone. Some date back to the early 1900s.

The Face of the River. Photo credit: Sierra Adare.

We make camp on the south side of Bowknot Bend, a nine mile loop in the river that takes you back to within 600 yards of its beginning. While Powell's crew ate supper spread out on a beach in this vicinity, he noted, "We name this Labyrinth Canyon."

I dig a shallow pit in the terrace of sand at the base of the cliff, throw in some charcoal bricks, and light a fire. After I mix up the cornbread, I pour it into a greased cast iron dutch oven. Scraping some coals to the side with the shovel, I create a flat bed to set the pot on. The piled up coals then get shoveled evenly (for uniform baking) onto the lid of the dutch oven.

Since heat rises and the bottom will cook quicker, I

maintain a hotter fire on the lid, adding more coals as they burn to ash. When the bread browns around the edge and the center bounces back when lightly touched, it's ready.

Powell's cook called his dutch oven an "iron bake-oven" and used it primarily for biscuits.

Day Two Dinner Recipes:

Green Chile Relleno
1–27 oz. can whole green chiles
1 lb. Monterey Jack cheese, sliced
1 1/2 c. flour
2 eggs
3/4 c. beer
2 c. plus 1 T. olive oil
1–28 oz. can whole tomatoes
1 T. cinnamon
    Pack each item separately. Beer doesn't need to be cold. Put oil in plastic bottle.

Blue Corn Bread
1 c. blue cornmeal
2/3 c. flour
1/4 c. powdered milk
1 T. sugar
1 t. baking powder
1 t. salt
1/2 t. baking soda
1–4 oz. can chopped green chiles
1 T. margarine
    Mix first 7 ingredients together and bag. Pack chiles and margarine separately.

Grapes

Pick firm, fresh grapes. Wash and remove from the stem. Pat dry and store in a zipper bag.

In the field preparation

Add undrained 4 oz. can of chopped peppers and 1 c. water to dry cornbread ingredients. Melt margarine in skillet. Spread dough in skillet. Bake with a lid fire for 30 minutes.

Heat oil in large pot. Open whole chiles and drain. Stuff with cheese.

Mix flour, eggs, beer, and 1 T. oil together. Dip chiles one at a time in the batter, completely coating them. Fry in oil until brown, flipping once. Repeat until all chiles are cooked.

Open tomatoes and pour into smaller pot. Roughly chop with the knife. Add cinnamon and bring to a boil. Serve over the stuffed peppers.

Serve grapes for dessert.

THIS MEAL requires no adaptation for horse or goat trips. To make the Chile Relleno suitable for backpacking, make them in the form of pancakes. Dehydrate chopped chiles, omit eggs, replace beer with 1/3 c. powdered milk and water, replace oil with 2 T. melted margarine to be used in the batter and 2 T. to fry the cakes in. Replace canned tomatoes with 4 fresh ones that have been chopped and dried. Replace grapes with raisins.

DAY THREE

BREAKFAST

Labyrinth Eggs
Coffee

LUNCH

Peanut butter and chopped sweet pickles sandwiches
Pineapple (canned, crushed) with
Chopped pecans sandwiches
Juice or soda

DINNER

Outlaw Stew
Bowknot

DAY THREE

> *July 15—There is an exquisite charm in our ride today down this beautiful canyon. It gradually grows deeper with every mile of travel; the walls are symmetrically curved and grandly arched, of a beautiful color, and reflected in the quiet waters in many places so as almost to deceive the eye and suggest to the beholder the thought that he is looking into profound depths. We are all in fine spirits and feel very gay, and the badinage of men is echoed from wall to wall. Now and then we whistle or shout or discharge a pistol, to listen to the reverberations among the cliffs.*
>
> —John Wesley Powell

While I prepare breakfast, Ron leads the party up on top of the Bowknot for a bird's-eye-view of the huge bend in the river.

One of the times Powell's crew awaited his return from an exploratory jaunt, they succeeded in catching a good, but unmentioned number of fish. "This is a delightful addition to our *menu*," the leader logged less than a month into the trip. I wonder if his stressing the word "menu" came as a result of the men tiring of the rations.

Day Three Breakfast Recipe:

Labyrinth Eggs
8 eggs
1–1.58 oz. tube anchovy paste
1–16 oz. can tomato sauce
2 T. pepper

2 T. parsley flakes
4 English muffins
    Pack each item separately.

In the field preparation
    Warm English muffin halves while boiling water for coffee by placing them on the lid of the water pot (or in the skillet with a two-burner stove). Heat skillet. Break eggs into it. Add 1/4 c. water. Cover and steam over medium heat until eggs are cooked.
    Spread anchovy paste over the English muffins. Top each half with an egg, Pour tomato sauce over egg. Sprinkle with pepper and parsley. Serve.
    THIS MEAL needs no adaptation for horse or goat trips, or for backpacking if you take the eggs in a special container and don't mind the extra weight.

    We get underway, but within half an hour a cold rain lashes us, falling in heavy sheets. The surface of the river rings with droplets. No immediate spot presents itself for us to land and dig slickers out of the dry bags. Then Lance glimpses a sliver-sized sandbar at the base of a cliff. We angle over to it and beach the boats. Of course, by the time we don our slickers and get back on the water, the rain quits.
    As we paddle through Canyonlands, the enormity of time soaks into my bones. With patient perseverance and endurance the river has cut its way through 1,000 feet of rock. The walls look like temples on crumbling foundations. Blind arches abound, created by rain seeping into tiny crevices in the cliffs, gnawing away the stone bit by bit until entire slabs break free and crash into talus fields at the wall's footing or get swallowed up by the river below.

Blind arches in Canyonlands. Photo credit: Sierra Adare.

By lunch time, the sun glitters off the water like thousands of fireflies. Cottonwoods hang over the bank, their delicate green leaves dancing in the current.

We put in at Mineral Canyon Bottoms and enjoy a picnic at the head of a draw that meanders into the side canyon. During the 1950s, a commercial uranium mine basked in the post World War II boom. Burros and wagons hauled out ten tons of ore over one of the few access roads into the lower canyon area, an iffy four-wheel drive, high-ground clearance kind of road these days. Now, only some rusted relics remain as reminders of this era.

Tonight we camp on a large, elongated island at Fort Bottom. Once we unload the gear and set up camp, we all pile into a couple of the canoes and cross to the "mainland" to explore the historic sites found there.

It's an easy climb up a dusty, nondescript path to "Outlaw Cabin." Rumor places it as a way station for the infamous Butch Cassidy. This inconspicuous log cabin, posing as a homesteader's abode, sits on a bench across the river from the once well-used trail leading to Brown's Hole or Hole-in-the-Wall.

On the pinnacle above the cabin stands a lookout tower believed to be built over a century before by Fremont Indians. The structure is constructed entirely out of native, flat stones laid with no mortar to hold them together. Two small circular rooms remain intact, with part of a third still visible.

The sun starts to set, bathing the landscape in fiery reds and oranges. Crickets begin their nightly rhapsody as we glide back to the island and a dinner of Outlaw Stew.

After a similar excursion, Powell wrote, "Now we return to camp. While eating supper we very naturally speak of better fare, as musty bread and spoiled bacon are not palatable."

Day Three Dinner Recipes:

Outlaw Stew

1/2 lb. bacon
3 potatoes
2 onions
6 carrots
1 t. pepper
2 T. parsley flakes

Pack bacon and carrots in ice chest for day three. Store onions and potatoes in net bags. Pack pepper shaker and a bag of parsley.

Bowknot

5 c. crisp rice cereal
2 c. miniature marshmallows

3/4 c. candied fruits

2 T. margarine

Bag each item separately.

In the field preparation

Lay strips of bacon in the bottom of the skillet, covering it. Slice vegetables. Put a layer of potato on top of the bacon. Sprinkle on some pepper and parsley. Add a layer of onion, then a layer of carrots. Repeat until all ingredients are used. Pour 3 c. water over the top. Cover and bring to a boil. Simmer 30 minutes or until potatoes and bacon are cooked. Do not stir. Add water if necessary to keep from burning. Serve.

While stew cooks (if you have a two-burner stove along), melt 1 T. margarine in a large pot. Add marshmallows, stirring until melted. Stir in cereals and fruit. Coat skillet with 1 T. margarine. Spread marshmallow mixture in skillet. Allow to set up for 10 minutes. Cut and serve.

AS AN OPTION on backpacking trips, cook, dry, and crumble bacon. Dehydrate potatoes, onions, and carrots. On horse and goat trips, this meal is suitable as is for the first day. If you plan to use it later in the trip, substitute canned or dried bacon.

DAY FOUR

BREAKFAST

Potatoes Canyonlands
Coffee

LUNCH

Baked beans mashed with catsup
Salmon (canned) with tomato slices and Dijon mustard
Fruit
Juice or soda

DINNER

Stillwater Spaghetti
White Rim Oranges

DAY FOUR

*July 17—We are now down among the
buttes, and in a region the surface of which
is naked, solid rock—a beautiful red sandstone, forming a smooth, undulating pave-
ment. The Indians call this the* Toom'pin
Tuweap', *or "Rock Land," and sometimes
the* Toom'pin wunear' Tuweap', *or "Land of
Standing Rock." Off to the south we see a
butte in the form of a fallen cross. It is several miles away, but it presents no inconspicuous figure on the landscape and must
be many hundreds of feet high, probably
more than 2,000. We note its position on
our map and name it "The Butte of the
Cross."*

—John Wesley Powell

The luxury of fresh fruit on a float trip was inconceivable
in 1869. Even dehydrated, fruits faired poorly. "The few
pounds of dried apples have been spread in the sun and
reshrunken to their normal [dried] bulk," wrote Powell after
their apples get soaked in the river.

Day Four Breakfast Recipe:

Potatoes Canyonlands
1 lb. turkey sausage
4 potatoes
6 green onions, chopped
1 apple
1–29 oz. can tomato sauce
1/2 t. cayenne pepper
1 T. margarine

Brown sausage. Dehydrate sausage and onions. Bag with cayenne pepper. Store potatoes, apple, tomato sauce, and margarine separately.

In the field preparation

Rehydrate sausage mixture. Melt margarine in a skillet. Grate potatoes. Saute potatoes with sausage and onion. Chop apple. Add to the sausage. When done, add tomato sauce. Serve.

THIS MEAL needs no adaptation on horse or goat trips. For backpacking, replace canned tomato sauce with 2 chopped and dried fresh tomatoes.

The Butte of the Cross dominates the vista for many miles before we reach it at lunchtime. We drift past it, the canoes nested together while we eat.

Then the unthinkable happens. We hear the unmistakable rush of white water, and our hearts start pounding. Our river guidebook says nothing about rough water ahead, and Ron's forehead creases in a deep frown. We scramble to untangle the canoes and paddle through a corridor of buff-colored cliff walls straining to touch the sky.

It's a false alarm. The cliffs have captured the sound of rifles and small haystacks (disturbances in the water caused by rocks beneath the surface) and bounce the noise up and down the canyon until we're sure we face uncharted white water within the confines of Stillwater Canyon. It makes us realize the thrill and the terror Powell and his men must have experienced.

We make an early day of it, putting in on the beach at Valentine Bottom. Above the sandy shore, bands of rusted sandstone and shale fade into the White Rim, the local name for the uppermost fringe of sandstone in Stillwater Canyon.

Once we set up camp, we eagerly dig into the crunchy canned vegetables in our Stillwater Spaghetti.

For want of some vegetables, the 1869 expedition gathered some "potato tops" from an Indian trader's garden, thinking the greens might make a nice change from their "salt-meat fare." "We stop and cook our greens for dinner; but soon one after another of the party is taken sick," Powell noted, finding out the hard way that only the tubers are edible.

Day Four Dinner Recipes:

Stillwater Spaghetti
1 lb. beef, sliced thin
10 mushrooms, sliced
2 stalks celery, chopped
1 bell pepper, chopped
3 T. Chinese Hot Mustard
1 beef bouillon cube
1–5 oz. can bamboo shoots
1–5 oz. can sliced water chestnuts
1/2–7 oz. pkg. rice sticks
Marinate meat in the mustard that has been thinned with 3 T. of water. Dehydrate meat, mushrooms, bell pepper, and celery. Bag together with bouillon cube. Pack bamboo shoots, chestnuts, and rice sticks.

White Rim Oranges
4 oranges
1–2 oz. pkg. almond slivers
1 c. sugar
8 graham crackers
Store each item separately.

In the field preparation

Rehydrate meat mixture. Bring to a boil with 1 c. water in a covered pot. Add bamboo shoots and chestnuts. Simmer, stirring frequently until everything is tender.

Meanwhile, bring another pot of water to boil. Add rice sticks. Cook for three minutes. Drain. Serve meat mixture over rice sticks.

Peel oranges and chop three of them. Squeeze the juice from the fourth one into the smaller pot, reserving pulp to chop and add with the rest. Dissolve sugar in the juice. Bring to a boil, stirring constantly until sugar mixture thickens and boils. Add oranges and almonds. Return to a boil. Boil 2 minutes, stirring constantly. Divide graham crackers and crush into the small bowls. Pour oranges over them and serve.

AS AN OPTION on backpack trips, dehydrate canned vegetables. If you don't wish to carry the extra weight of the oranges, choose another lightweight dessert. For horse and goat trips, no adaptation is required.

DAY FIVE

BREAKFAST

Lazy Water Cereal
Fruit
Coffee

LUNCH

Hard boiled eggs with stewed tomatoes
Lady of the Lake Lunch
Juice or soda

DINNER

Turk's Head Ham
Cherry Challenger
Tea

DAY FIVE

July 17—When thinking of these rocks one must not conceive of piles of boulders or heaps of fragments, but of a whole land of naked rock, with giant forms carved on it: cathedral-shaped buttes, towering hundreds or thousands of feet, cliffs that cannot be sealed, and canyon walls that shrink the river into insignificance, with vast, hollow domes and tall pinnacles and shafts set on the verge overhead; and all highly colored— buff, gray, red, brown, and chocolate—never lichened, never moss-covered, but bare, and often polished.

—John Wesley Powell

Powell found it necessary to cache food along the route, where possible. A cave near a creek that fed into the Green provided one such reserve. When the men arrived at it, they found a party of Indians had been camped close to the cache for several weeks and worried that their supplies would no longer be there. "Our fears are soon allayed, for find the cache undisturbed," Powell wrote upon returning to camp.

Day Five Breakfast Recipe:

Lazy Water Cereal
assorted boxes of cereal
2–12 oz. cans evaporated milk
    Bag in your usual serving sizes. Pack cans of milk.

In the field preparation
    While water boils for coffee, open milk and mix with water until desired drinking consistency (no more than equal

parts of milk and water). Pour cereal in bowls. Add milk. Serve with assorted fruits.

THIS MEAL needs no adaptation for horse or goat trips. For backpacking, substitute powdered milk and dried fruit.

In 1869, the water flowed faster through Stillwater Canyon. "Late in the afternoon," Powell recorded, "the water becomes swift and our boats make great speed."

On the other hand, we creep along, spending the morning and most of the afternoon linked together, content to drift.

The day is desert hot, the sun relentless. We guzzle cans of fruit juice and get into paddle fights, batting dirty water on each other as a cooling down strategy. Bobby and Alan stage a mock sword fight with their paddle handles, almost tipping their canoe over as they duck and lunge at each other.

Lunch offers a welcome break as it did for Powell's team. While tied together, drifting, they often read from Scott's *Lady of the Lake.* We read excerpts from Powell's trip instead.

Day Five Lunch Recipe:

Lady of the Lake Lunch
2–2 oz. cans anchovies
3 T. Chinese Hot Mustard
1/4 t. cayenne pepper
1 T. parsley flakes
2 T. margarine

Bag cayenne and parsley together. Store remaining ingredients separately.

In the field preparation
Open anchovies and empty into a bowl. Mash with a fork. Add remaining ingredients and stir until smooth. Spread over crackers, bread, bagels, or muffins. Serve.

THIS LUNCH needs no adaptation for horse or goat trips, or for backpacking provided you don't mind the extra weight and serve it over crackers.

Rock formations known as Challenger (left), Sphinx (center), and Turk's Head (right).
Photo credit: Sierra Adare.

Later in the day, when the current picks up a little, we pull out of our lethargy and separate the canoes. The scenery also livens up. Rock formations such as "The Sphinx" perch high above the water.

Turk's Head, a stone variation on a headdress straight out of the movie *Lawrence of Arabia,* and an unnamed pinnacle we dub "Challenger," (because it looks surprisingly like the space shuttle ready for launch) flank the Sphinx.

As the canoe glides past this majestic work of Nature, I glance back for one last look. But from this direction, Sphinx has transformed itself into Snoopy. That's the funny thing with wind and weather sculptures. Perspective changes them entirely.

Beyond the bend from the Sphinx and its companions, campsites get scarce. Cliffs rise 1,300 feet above the water. Neither Powell nor Dellenbaugh wrote anything about this section of the river. However, George Y. Bradley, who accompanied Powell's first expedition, called this segment of Canyonlands "dark and threatening."

At the entrance to Horse Canyon, we point the canoes at the shore and call it a day. After a short hike up a well-defined animal trail, we discover what must have been an old Indian camp ground, littered with flakes and bits of worked jasper. Surrounded by rim rock, our location commands an extensive view of the river, as well as back into the canyon.

While the guys haul the sleeping gear up top, Erin helps me set up the kitchen down by the delta of the stream that runs in the bottom of the canyon. Insects swarm everywhere. Bats, too. Ron builds a fire so the smoke will keep the mosquitos away while we eat.

One campfire Powell's men started brought disaster to the expedition. A whirlwind came up and scattered the fire among some dead willows nearby. The men dashed for the boats, grabbing as much gear as they could carry. "The cook fills his arms with the mess-kit, and jumping into a boat, stumbles and falls, and away go our cooking utensils into the river," stated Powell in the log. "Our plates are gone; our spoons are gone; our knives and forks are gone."

To top it off, the bank of willows that hung over the boats caught fire, forcing the men to cut the crafts loose. The swift-flowing water propelled them downstream over a rapid filled with rocks. When the men finally managed to steer the boats ashore again and hiked back to the site of the fire, all they found were "a few tin cups, basins, and a camp kettle; and this is all the mess-kit we now have."

Day Five Dinner Recipes:

Turk's Head Ham
1 c. ground ham
1 large onion, diced
2 green chiles, chopped
8 mushrooms, sliced
2 large tomatoes, chopped
1/2 bell pepper, chopped
1 t. cumin
1 t. parsley flakes
1 T. margarine
1 recipe Wild Side Rice (see Index)
    Dehydrate ham, vegetables, mushrooms, and tomatoes.
Bag with parsley and cumin. Dry rice according to the recipe.

Cherry Challenger
1–20 oz. can pineapple rings in juice
1–16 oz. can peach halves in juice
1–16 oz. jar maraschino cherries
1/4 c. coconut flakes
    Transfer cherries to plastic zipper bag. Bag coconut. Pack
cans of fruit.

In the field preparation
    Hydrate ham mixture while water boils for hot drinks.
Place ham mixture and 2 c. cold water in a big pot. Cover.
Bring to a boil over high heat. Add margarine. Lower heat and
simmer 15 minutes or until food is tender. Add enough water
to make 1 1/2 c. of liquid. Return to a boil. Stir in dried rice.
Remove from heat. Allow mixture to sit for 10 minutes before
serving. Wrap an ensolite pad around the pot to keep it warm.
Reheat a few minutes if it cools too quickly.
    Divide pineapple rings among the small bowls, reserving

juice. Next divide the cherries, then the peach halves, reserving peach juice. Mix the two juices. Pour over fruit. Sprinkle coconut on top. Serve.

AS AN OPTION on backpacking trips, dehydrate chopped green chiles and serve dried fruit for dessert. For horse or goat trips, this meal needs no adaptation.

DAY SIX

BREAKFAST

Fruit Confluence
White Water Biscuits
Coffee

LUNCH

Apricots (canned) mashed with chopped walnuts
Smoked Sausages mashed with Salsa Verde
Juice or soda

DINNER

Powell Potato Chowder
Green River Vegetable Medley
Jasper Springs Cake
Tea

DAY SIX

> *July 20—The course of the Green at this point is approximately at right angles to that of the Colorado, and on the brink of the latter canyon we find the same system of terraced and walled glens. The walls and pinnacles and towers are of sandstone, homogeneous in structure but not in color, as they show broad bands of red, buff, and gray.*
>
> —John Wesley Powell

Not all of Powell's food entries involved hardship. When a string of bad luck looked like it might end the expedition, the 1869 group stumbled upon a man and his two sons scouting a location for a town on the river bank. They sent a messenger to a town twenty miles up the valley. The next day a wagon arrived with a cornucopia of supplies and a rare treat — "two or three dozen melons."

Day Six Breakfast Recipes:

Fruit Confluence
1 honeydew melon
1–20 oz. can pineapple in juice
2 oranges
2 bananas
1/2 c. chopped dates
1/2 c. chopped walnuts
2–6 oz. containers custard style strawberry yogurt
Bag dates and nuts together. Pack remaining ingredients. (Choose an under-ripe melon so it will ripen during the trip and be just right on day six.) Store yogurt in the ice chest.

White Water Biscuits

2 c. flour
4 T. powdered buttermilk
1 t. salt
1 t. baking powder
1 t. baking soda
3 T. margarine
    Blend and bag all ingredients except margarine.

In the field preparation

Cut margarine into biscuit mix. Add 1 1/4 c. of cold water to dry ingredients or enough to form a soft dough. Pat into biscuits about 1/2 inch thick. Bake in the skillet with a lid fire 10–15 minutes until lightly browned. Makes 12–14.

Open the pineapple, draining liquid (reserve it to add to tea for a different flavor). Peel and chop melon, oranges, and bananas. In the large pot, mix all ingredients. Stir well and serve.

THIS MEAL is only suitable as a first day horse or goat trip breakfast.

From Horse Canyon, it's an easy float to the confluence of the Green and Colorado rivers. So we take a long lunch break at Jasper Canyon, exploring it. Brush grows thick at the mouth of the draw, forcing us to bushwhack our way through.

Jasper Springs Creek meanders through the canyon floor. We follow it. Fossilized crab and worm tracks decorate limestone chunks that litter the bank. Then the creek opens into an amphitheater of rim rock. Water spills over the edge, falling into a pool three hundred feet below. An irresistible spot for an afternoon dip, we strip down to our swim suits and wade in. Sun warmed, the clear water creates a luxurious, refreshing sensation.

An hour passes, then two. None of us wish to leave, but

we want to make the confluence before dark. So we retrace
our steps and climb back into the boats.

The White Rim of Stillwater Canyon turns into a series
of grotesque rock formations as we float nearer to the confluence. Cliffs a thousand feet high tower above us, binding us
within the narrow confines of the river. Stone outcroppings
that resemble surreal-shaped birds with serrated beaks and
gouged eyes stare down on us.

When the walls give way to the "Y" of the confluence
and a wide sandbar just around the bend on the Colorado, I
feel a sense of anti-climax. Two grand rivers come together
after flowing through incredible walls of rock. They comingle
more mud and silt than water and gurgle along as if the separate rivers never existed.

As we beach the canoes I notice fresh deer prints in the
wet sand.

The 1869 party stopped to hunt whenever they spotted
game in an area where they could bring the boats ashore. One
hunt resulted in a feast. "And a feast it is!" Powell exclaimed
in his log. "Two fine young [mountain] sheep! We care not for
bread or beans or dried apples to-night; coffee and mutton are
all we ask."

Our last-night-on-the-river feast differs from Powell's,
but we enjoy it with the same excitement he expressed.

Day Six Dinner Recipes:

Powell Potato Chowder
1–10 oz. can baby clams in water
5 potatoes
1 onion
10 mushrooms, sliced thin
1 T. parsley flakes
1/2 t. thyme

1 t. pepper
1/2 c. powdered milk
1 t. salt
2 T. margarine
    Dehydrate mushrooms. Bag them together with parsley, thyme, pepper, milk, and salt. Store onion and potatoes in net bags. Pack canned clams. Store margarine separately.

Green River Vegetable Medley

2 yellow squash, sliced
20 okra, chopped
1 cucumber, sliced
12 mushrooms, sliced
2 t. thyme
2 T. soy sauce
2 T. margarine
    Dehydrate vegetables and bag together with the thyme. Store soy sauce in a small plastic bottle. Keep margarine separate.

Jasper Springs Cake

2 c. flour
2 T. sugar
1 t. baking powder
1 t. ground cloves
1 t. mace
1 t. cinnamon
1 c. raisins
1/2 c. honey
1 egg
1/4 c. plus 1 T. margarine
    Mix and bag first 7 ingredients. Put honey in a plastic bottle. Store margarine and egg in the ice chest.

In the field preparation

Rehydrate Green River Vegetable Medley and mushroom mixture for the chowder. Remove egg and margarine from the ice chest to warm up to outside temperature. Slice potatoes thin and chop onion.

Fill pot half full of water and pour in clams and juice. Add potatoes, onion, mushroom mixture, and 2 T. margarine. Cover and bring to a boil over high heat. Reduce heat to low and continue to cook until potatoes are done, stirring occasionally.

Meanwhile, pour vegetables into the skillet. Add soy sauce, 2 T. margarine, and enough water to cover the bottom of the skillet. Cover. Steam until vegetables are tender, 10–15 minutes. Add more water as needed.

Melt 1 T. margarine in skillet and set aside. Beat 1/4 c. margarine and sugar together in large pot. Add egg, then honey, then 1/2 c. water, beating well each time. Stir in flour mixture. When completely moistened, pour into skillet. Bake over low heat with a lid fire for 40–50 minutes.

THIS MEAL needs no adaptation for horse or goat trips. For backpacking, dehydrate clams.

DAY SEVEN

BREAKFAST

Last Day Lyonnaise
Tea

LUNCH

Peanut butter with chopped dates
Raisins chopped with orange sections
Juice or soda

DINNER

Dellenbaugh's Anvil
Ricochet Bars
Tea

DAY SEVEN

> *July 18—The day is spent in obtaining the*
> *time and spreading our rations, which we*
> *find are badly injured. The flour has been*
> *wet and dried so many times that it is all*
> *musty and full of hard lumps. We make a*
> *sieve of mosquito netting and run our flour*
> *through it, losing more than 200 pounds by*
> *the process.*
>
> —John Wesley Powell

Satisfaction and sadness stir in camp this morning. Unlike Powell's expedition which continued until November 1, 1869, today our journey ends with a sixty mile jet boat trip up the Colorado to Moab. We scatter in different directions at sunrise to say personal good-byes to the river.

Breakfast is, as Powell wrote on the day three of his men mutinied (unable to stand the treacherous rapids and lack of food any longer), "as solemn as a funeral."

Day Seven Breakfast Recipe:

Last Day Lyonnaise
4 eggs
1 small onion
1 clove garlic
3 T. margarine
1 T. flour
2 T. parsley flakes
1/4 c. powdered milk
4 bagels

Bag milk and parsley. Put onion and garlic in a net bag. Store remaining ingredients separately.

In the field preparation

Put eggs in large pot of water. Cover and bring to a boil over high heat, warming bagels on top of the lid (or in the skillet over low heat with a two-burner stove). Boil 10 minutes and remove from heat.

Meanwhile, chop onion and garlic. Melt margarine in the skillet. Add 1 c. water to milk and mix. Set aside. Saute onion and garlic in margarine for 1 minute over high heat, stirring constantly. Add flour. Stir until absorbed. Add milk. Stir and heat over medium until gravy bubbles and thickens. Cover and set aside. Peel eggs, reserving water for tea. Chop eggs and add to gravy. Serve over bagels.

THIS MEAL needs no adaptation for horse or goat trips. (However, since bagels will turn moldy after a few days without refrigeration, serve early in the trip.) For backpacking, take only if you don't mind the extra weight.

I stocked a full set of meals for the seventh day even though we'd arranged for the jet boat to meet us this morning. Afternoon arrives. The boat doesn't. Engine problems delay it until late in the day. The extra food means we don't need to ration supplies like Powell did in this same spot "for it became evident that we would run short of food before we could get any more," he noted.

Day Seven Dinner Recipes:

Dellenbaugh's Anvil
1/2 lb. turkey sausage
1 eggplant, chopped
2 large tomatoes, chopped
1/2 bell pepper, chopped
1 onion, chopped
1 T. black pepper

2 T. margarine

3 c. egg noodles

Brown sausage. Dry meat, eggplant, tomatoes, bell pepper, and onion. Bag meat and onion together. Bag vegetables, tomatoes, and black pepper. Bag egg noodles separately.

Ricochet Bars

1 c. flour

1 t. baking powder

1 t. salt

1 T. Amaretto flavored coffee drink

1/2 c. nuts, chopped

1/2 c. miniature marshmallows

1/2 c. semi-sweet chocolate chips

1/3 c. molasses

1 egg

5 T. margarine

Mix and bag together the first five ingredients. Bag marshmallows and chocolate chips together. Pack a plastic container of molasses. Store egg and margarine separately.

In the field preparation

Fill a pot with cold water. Cover and bring to a boil over high head. Reconstitute meat and vegetables in bags on the lid while water comes to a boil. Remove pot from stove. Make hot drinks with half the water. Insulate the remaining water by wrapping an ensolite pad around the pot to keep it warm. Melt 2 T. margarine in the skillet over high heat. Add meat. Cover and cook until tender, adding water as it becomes absorbed. Add vegetables and a cup of cold water. Bring to a boil, adding enough water to maintain about a cup of liquid in the bottom of the skillet. Boil for two minutes. Remove from heat and keep warm. Return the pot of water to the stove. Over high heat, bring to boil again. Add egg noodles and cook until tender. Serve sausage/vegetable mixture over drained noodles.

Melt margarine in the skillet. In a pot combine 5 T. margarine, molasses, and egg. Stir in flour mixture and spread in the skillet. Top with marshmallows and chocolate chips. Bake over low heat with a lid fire for 15–20 minutes. Cut and serve.

THIS MEAL needs no adaptation for backpacking, horse or goat trips.

One of many ways to get to the trail. Photo credit: Wyoming Travel Commission.

GETTING TO THE TRAIL

Write or call the state where you plan to backpack, goatpack, horsepack, or take a float trip for a Vacation Guide. Ask for additional outfitter information.

Colorado Vacation Guide
Colorado Tourism Board
P.O. Box 38700
Denver, CO 80238
1-800-433-2656

Idaho State Vacation Guide
Idaho Dept. of Commerce
700 W. State St.
P.O. Box 83720
Boise, ID 83720–0093
1–800–847–4843

Montana Travel Planner
Dept. of Commerce
1424 9th Ave.
Helena, MT 59620
1–800–VISIT MT
or in state 406–444–2654

Nevada Vacation Guide
Nevada State Board of
Tourism
600 E. Williams #207
Carson City, NV 89710
1–800–NEVADA–8

New Mexico Vacation Guide
New Mexico Dept. of
Tourism
1100 St. Francis Dr.
Joseph Montoya Bldg.
Santa Fe, NM 87503
1–800–545–2040

Oregon Vacation Guide
Oregon State Board of
Tourism
Eco. Development Dept.
595 Cottage St. NE
Salem, OR 97310
800–547–7842 or
800–543–8838

Utah Vacation Guide
Utah Board of Tourism
Council Hall, Capitol Hill
Salt Lake City, UT 84114
801–538–1030

Washington Vacation Guide
101 General Admin. Bldg.
Olympia, WA 98504
206–753–5600

Wyoming Vacation Guide
Wyoming Division of
Tourism
I–25 at College Dr.
Cheyenne, WY 82002
1–800–225–5996

A historical perspective of the outdoor eating experience.
Photo credit: Hot Springs County Museum Cultural Center.

HISTORICAL BIBLIOGRAPHY

A Country Kitchen, 1850. Maynard, MA: Chandler Press, 1987.

Back, Joe. *Horses, Hitches & Rocky Trails: "The Packers Bible."* Boulder, CO: Johnson Books, 1987.

Butruille, Susan G. *Women's Voices from the Oregon Trail.* Boise, ID: Tamarack Books, 1993.

Child, Lydia M. *The American Frugal Housewife.* Bedford, MA: Applewood Books, 1832.

Coyle, L. Patrick Jr. *The World Encyclopedia of Food.* New York: Facts On File, 1982.

Delano, A. *Life on the Plains and at the Diggings.* Buffalo, NY: Miller, Orton & Mulligan, 1854.

Dellenbaugh, Frederick S. *The Romance of the Colorado River: The*

Story of its Discovery in 1540, with an Account of the Later Explorations, and with Special Reference to the Voyages of Powell through the Line of the Great Canyons. New York: G.P. Putnam's Sons, 1902.

Grinnell, George B. *The Cheyenne Indians: Their History and Ways of Life.* Vols. 1 and 2. Lincoln, NE: University of Nebraska Press, 1923.

Hamilton, William T. *My Sixty Years on the Plains.* New York: Knickerbocker Press, 1905.

Hartwell, Marcia B. *A Sampler of Recipes 1796 to 1908.* Northampton, MA: Hartwell, 1984.

Kalman, Bobbie. *Food for the Settler.* New York: Crabtree Publishing Co., 1982.

Lee, Hilde G. *Taste of the States: A Food History of America.* Charlottesville, VA: Howell Press, 1992.

Marcy, Randolph B. *The Prairie Traveler.* Old Saybrook, CT: Applewood Books, 1859.

Miller, Alfred J. *The West of Alfred Jacob Miller.* Ed. Marvin C. Ross. Norman, OK: University of Oklahoma Press, 1968.

Powell, J.W. *The Exploration of the Colorado River and Its Canyons.* New York: Dover Publications, reprinted 1961.

Reedstrom, Ernest L. *Historic Dress of the Old West.* New York: Blandford Press, 1986.

Rickey, Don. *Forty Miles A Day On Beans and Hay.* Norman, OK: University of Oklahoma Press, 1963.

Riggs, Stephen R. *Mary and I: Forty Years with the Sioux.* Williamstown, MA: Corner House Publishers, reprinted 1971.

Roast, Waverly and Richard de Rochemont. *Eating in America: A History.* New York: William Morrow & Co., 1976.

Trenholm, Virginia C., and Maurine Carley. *The Shoshonis: Sentinels of the Rockies.* Norman, OK: University of Oklahoma Press, 1964.

Walker, Mrs. Elkanah and Mrs. Cushing Eells. *First White Women Over the Rockies: Diaries, Letters, and Biographical Sketches of the Six Women of the Oregon Mission who made the Overland Journey in 1836 and 1838.* Vols. 1, 2, and 3. Glendale, CA: Arthur H. Clark Co., 1963.

Webber, Bert, ed. *Diary of Jane Gould in 1862.* Medford, OR: Webb Research Group, Publishers, 1993.

Williams, Mary L., ed. *An Army Wife's Cookbook With Household Hints and Home Remedies.* Tucson, AZ: Southwest Parks and Monuments Association, 1972.

Zwinger, Ann. *Run River, Run: A Naturalist's Journey Down One of the Great Rivers of the West.* New York: Harper & Row. Publishers, 1975.

Goat camp in the Honeycombs. Photo credit: Jeff Corney.

INDEX

ABOUT THE AUTHOR

Photo Credit: Jeff Corney

Sierra Adare grew up with the wilderness as her backyard. The concept for *Backcountry Cooking* came about while on a backpacking expedition where she had signed on as the cook. When she questioned the other participants about their food preferences, the hikers comments ranged from "no macs and cheese, please" to "no space food" (prepackaged "meals" from the backpacking store). "Since I like to eat real food in the backcountry," Adare admits, "I created recipes for dishes such as Chile Relleno, Turkey Eggplant Parmesan, and Blueberry Pie. Nobody believed they could get such dishes in the wilderness. Or how easy they were to prepare in the backcountry."

Adare's cooking, travel, and how-to articles have appeared in both regional and national publications. Included among her published credits are *Persimmon Hill, Wild West Magazine, Roundup Magazine, Byline, Trilogy Magazine, Mother Earth News, Country Magazine, Farmstead Magazine, Denver Post, Casper Star Tribune,* as well as newspaper columns.

In addition to her award-winning book, *What Editors Look For: How to Write Compelling Queries, Cover Letters, Synopses & Book Proposals,* and *Jackson Hole Uncovered,* she has contributed to five other books.

Adare lectures and presents workshops in cooking, writing, and marketing, as well as teaching cooking and writing classes for Central Wyoming College.

Active in several organizations, Adare is a member of Western Writers of America, Wordcraft Circle of Native American Writers and Storytellers, Wyoming Writers, the Western History Association, and Women Writing the West.

From her home at the base of the Wind River Range, she skis, skydives, and sails, in addition to hiking, horsepacking and horseback riding, goatpacking, canoeing, ballooning, and car-camping.

The author welcomes comments and suggestions for subsequent editions of *Backcountry Cooking*. Please write c/o Tamarack Books, PO Box 190313, Boise, ID 83719-0313.

Additional copies of *Backcountry Cooking* can be found in fine bookstores nationwide or directly from the publisher.

If ordering direct, please include a check for $19.95 (book @ $16.95 plus a shipping/handling charge of $3.00). Idaho residents should send $20.80 (book @ $16.95, shipping/handling $3.00, and Idaho tax $.85).

Send your name, address, and check to:

Backcountry Cooking Orders
Tamarack Books, Inc.
PO Box 190313
Boise, ID 83719-0313

To place orders using MasterCard or Visa,
please call 1–800–962–6657.

Write or call for a free catalog 1–800–962–6657.

KAPCO

DISCARD